Ellery H. Clark

Track Athletics up to Date

Salzwasser

Ellery H. Clark

Track Athletics up to Date

1. Auflage | ISBN: 978-3-84604-928-0

Erscheinungsort: Frankfurt, Deutschland

Erscheinungsjahr: 2020

Salzwasser Verlag GmbH

Reprint of the original, first published in 1920.

TRACK ATHLETICS
UP TO DATE

ELERY H. CLARK,
Former all-around amature champion of America.

Track Athletics Up To Date

BY

ELLERY H. CLARK

Physical Director, Browne & Nichols School, Cambridge, Mass.; Assistant Graduate
Treasurer, Harvard Athletic Association, 1915-1917; Winner of High and
Broad Jumps at Olympic Games, Athens, 1896; All-Around Athletic
Champion of New England, 1896, 1897, 1909, 1910; All-Around
Athletic Champion of America, 1897, 1903; Author of
"Reminiscences of an Athlete," and (in collab-
oration with John Graham) of "Prac-
tical Track and Field Athletics."

NEW YORK

DUFFIELD AND COMPANY

1920

To My Son
ELLERY H. CLARK, JR.

CONTENTS

PREFACE

There are many of us, at the present day, who are enthusiastic over sports on track and field. And yet, in spite of our interest, have we ever tried to study our subject systematically? Have we ever acquired more than a "fair general ignorance" regarding it?

To make my meaning clear, let us consider, by way of comparison, the familiar example of the attorney who is consulted upon a point of law. Rarely, if he is a man of experience, does he give his answer offhand, but, on the contrary, his first act is to consult the authorities and to read the decisions of the courts and the theories of the text writers on the point in question. Then, and then only, is he in a position to express an intelligent opinion upon the case.

It is this principle which I have borne in mind in writing the present volume. First, I have endeavored to trace, with brevity, the history of track athletics; next, I have noted some of the best of the many books, pamphlets and special articles which have been written on this subject; and lastly, I have tried to summarize, in the year 1919, our present knowledge of proper methods of training and of performing the various events on track and field.

The idea itself is, I think, sound, and, within its special field, not without novelty. Of the manner in which I have developed it, the reader, of course, must be the judge.

I desire to record here my sincere thanks to Mr. Michael J. Conroy, of the staff of the Boston Public Library, for his unfailing kindness in helping me to bring together the varied material upon which this book is based.

ELLERY H. CLARK.

Boston, September, 1919.

TRACK ATHLETICS
UP TO DATE

CHAPTER I

HISTORICAL

WHEN a young man decides to take part in track and field athletics—running, jumping and throwing the weights—it should interest him to know that these are sports not merely of modern origin, but that they date back to the earliest dawn of history. Thus Professor McKenzie tells us that "The survival of the cave man was determined by his ability to run fast, to leap far, and to throw straight, and we are apt to forget the value in modern life of the quick eye, the steady nerve, and the firm hand."[1] And similarly Montague Shearman, the English author, says that "Running and jumping are so natural and so easy to the young, that in one sense it may be said they no more have a history than laughing or weeping. As long as there have been men on the earth it may safely be asserted that there have been running matches; and in every warlike nation feats of strength, speed, and endurance of the body have excited admiration."[2]

These, of course, are general statements, but it is easy to illustrate them by concrete examples. Thus, in Greek literature, besides the many references to the Olympic Games, there is, in the Twenty-third Book of the Iliad, the famous narrative of the Funeral Games in honor of Patroclus, with the vivid picture of the foot race, where,

---

[1] Introduction, by Professor R. Tait McKenzie, to Michael C. Murphy's "Athletic Training." New York: Charles Scribner's Sons, 1914.
[2] "Athletics and Football," by Montague Shearman. The Badminton Library. London, 1887.

TRACK ATHLETICS UP TO DATE

as the modern "scribe" would doubtless phrase it, the wily
Ulysses "lays back and lets Ajax go out in front and make
the pace."

>   In due array
> They stood; Achilles showed the goal. At once
> Forward they sprang. Oïlean Ajax soon
> Gained on the rest, but close behind him ran
> The great Ulysses. As a shapely maid
> Flinging the shuttle draws with careful hand
> The thread that fills the warp, and so brings near
> The shuttle to her bosom, just so near
> To Ajax ran Ulysses, in the prints
> Made by his rival's feet, before the dust
> Fell back upon them. As he ran, his breath
> Smote on the head of Ajax. All the Greeks
> Shouted applause to him, encouraging
> His ardor for the victory;[3]

Moreover, at the same games there was also a contest
at putting the weight, which apparently, in these heroic
days, was much heavier than our modern "sixteen-pound
shot," or even than our massive "fifty-six."

> Again Pelides placed before the host
> A mass of iron, shapeless from the forge,
> Which once the strong Eëtion used to hurl;
> But swift Achilles, when he took his life,
> Brought it with other booty in his ships
> To Troas. Rising, he addressed the Greeks:—
> "Stand forth, whoever will contend for this,
> And if broad fields and rich be his, this mass
> Will last him many years. The man who tends
> His flocks, or guides his plough, need not be sent
> To town for iron: he will have it here."
> He spake, and warlike Polypoetes rose.
> Uprose the strong Leonteus, who in form
> Was like a god. The son of Telamon
> Rose also, and Epeius nobly born;
> Each took his place. Epeius seized the mass,
> And sent it whirling. All the Achaians laughed.
> The loved of Mars, Leonteus, flung it next,
> And after him the son of Telamon,

[3] The Iliad of Homer, translated by William Cullen Bryant: Boston,
Fields, Osgood & Co., 1870.

HISTORICAL

> The large-limbed Ajax, from his vigorous arm
> Sent it beyond the mark of both. But when
> The sturdy warrior Polypoetes took
> The mass in hand, as far as o'er his beeves
> A herdsman sends his whirling staff, so far
> This cast outdid the rest. A shout arose;
> The friends of sturdy Polypoetes took
> The prize, and bore it to the hollow ships.[4]

Again, in Latin literature, there is the record, in the Aeneid, of the games held upon the anniversary of the death of Anchises. Aeneas begins by making an announcement, precisely as we do today, to the effect that "Handsome prizes will be awarded to first, second and third in each event." Next, we are informed that two of the contestants, Nisus and Euryalus, were bosom friends; and then follows the spirited account of the foot race, unfortunately not run in "lanes."

> First, before all the rest,
> Flies Nisus, darting swifter than the wind,
> Or wingèd thunderbolt. Then Salius next
> Follows, but far behind; Euryalus
> The third in speed. Him follows Helymus.
> Now close behind, behold, Diores flies,
> Toe touching heel, and hangs upon his rear;
> And had more space remained, he would have passed,
> Or left the contest doubtful. Almost now
> The last stage was completed, and they neared
> With weary feet the goal, when Nisus slides
> Unhappily amid some slippery blood
> Of heifer slain, that, poured upon the ground,
> Had wet the grass. Pressing exultant on,
> The youth his foothold lost, and prone he falls
> Amid the sacred blood and filth impure.
> Yet not forgetful of Euryalus,
> And of their loves, he, in the slippery place,
> Rising, obstructs the way of Salius,
> Who, falling o'er him, sprawls upon the ground.
> On flies Euryalus, and, through his friend,
> Holds the first place, as 'mid the applauding shouts
> He runs. Then Helymus comes in, and next

[4] The Iliad of Homer, translated by William Cullen Bryant: Boston, Fields, Osgood & Co., 1870.

Diores, for the third. Here Salius fills
All the wide hollow of the assembled crowd,
And front seats of the fathers, with his cries,
Demanding that the prize should be restored,
Snatched from him by a trick. But favor smiles
For Euryalus, and his becoming tears;
And worth seems worthier in a lovely form.
Diores seconds him, and with loud voice
Declares that he in vain had striven to win
The last prize, if to Salius falls the first.
Then spoke Æneas: "Youths, your prizes all
Remain to you assured. No one may change
The order of the palm. But let me still
Pity a friend whose ill-luck merits not
Misfortune." Saying this, to Salius then
He gives a huge Gaetulian lion's skin
Heavy with rough hair, and with gilded claws.
Here Nisus spoke: "If such the prizes given
To those who lose, and falls win pity thus,
What boon worthy of Nisus wilt thou give?
I who deserved the first crown, had not chance
To me, as well as Salius, proved unkind."
And as he spoke, he showed his face and limbs
Smeared with the mud and filth. The good sire smiled,
And bade a shield be brought, the skilful work
Of Didymaon, taken by the Greeks
From Neptune's sacred door; this signal gift
Æneas to the worthy youth presents.[5]

This passage furnishes food for thought. At first, doubtless, we are disposed to criticize the ruling of Aeneas, and, according to present standards, there is surely something humorous in the description of Nisus, who so flagrantly "gave the elbow" to Salius, as "the worthy youth"; so that it is not surprising to find that a modern commentator views the whole affair with disgust, calls Aeneas an "ineffable prig," and claims that "outside of the police-court records nothing, for lack of chivalry, for contemptible meanness, for impudent self-assertion, equals this story of the foot-race at the anniversary of the funeral of Anchises."[6]

[5] The Aeneid of Virgil: Translated into English Blank Verse by C. P. Cranch. Houghton, Mifflin & Co., 1897.
[6] "The Ethics of Ancient and Modern Athletics": Price Collier, 32 Forum, 309.

HISTORICAL

And yet, upon reflection, while from a strictly competitive standpoint I of course quite agree with Mr. Collier, I am inclined to think that on the whole he is possibly a trifle too severe in his judgments. The games are, so to speak, a literary as well as an athletic event; not only Aeneas, but Virgil, must be reckoned with; and if, as is generally agreed, the first duty of the story teller is to interest his readers, then the Latin poet has scored an undoubted success. Again, I imagine that the Trojan leader scarcely regarded the whole incident as seriously as does Mr. Collier. In the mind of Aeneas, doubtless "the games were the thing"; it was in honor of Anchises that they were being held; and from this standpoint it was far more fitting to have them a success, and to see everyone satisfied, than to have the contestants indulge in unseemly wrangling over the winning or losing of a prize. Athletics, with us, have come to be such a life and death affair, that I believe, after all, we may properly study this classic foot race from more angles than one.

Nor were track athletics confined solely to the Greeks and Romans; there were Teutonic champions also. And thus, in the Nibelungenlied we read of Siegfried:

> Such was his skill and puissance, that none could come him near
> To hurl the stone tempestuous or dart the whizzing spear,[7]

while for real prowess with the weights Brunhilda seems fairly to be entitled to first honors, for when she "bar'd her arm of snow,"

> Then was the strength of Brunhild to each beholder shown.
> Into the ring by th' effort of panting knights a stone
> Was borne of weight enormous, massy and large and round.
> It strain'd twelve brawny champions to heave it to the ground.[8]

[7] "The Nibelungenlied," translated by W. N. Lettsom: New York, Scribner, 1903.
[8] Ibid.

And this stone she proceeded to "put" with the utmost ease, and naturally without much fear of successful competition. Surely, there was no suggestion of the "clinging vine" about Brunhilda.

Next, after this fair champion, to come directly to our English ancestors, I cannot recall, in Anglo-Saxon literature, any specific mention of track and field. It was on—and in—the sea that the Anglo-Saxon was most at home; and thus Beowulf, the hero of the "first English epic," who, in a contest of "ocean-endurance," swam for five days and nights, through

> Churning waves and chilliest weather,
> Darkling night and the northern wind,

was later conquered upon land by a dragon, a "murderous monster mad with rage," who breathed forth fire like a locomotive, and who swept across the evening sky like a Zeppelin on a raid.

It is, however, highly important to note that as far as antiquity goes, Irish athletics are apparently in a class of their own. John Boyle O'Reilly, poet and athlete, tells us of Cuchullin, or Cuchullain, who, long before the Olympic Games were thought of, was the All-around Champion of Ireland, A.M. 4480, and who performed, among other events, at the roth-cleas, or wheel feat, which was seemingly the direct forerunner of the modern hammer throw.[9] Further, Mr. O'Reilly describes the ancient games at Tailten and Carman, and similar information is given us by one who is both a mighty athlete and a great authority upon athletics, namely, Mr. James S. Mitchel, in his really noteworthy pamphlet entitled "How to Become a Weight Thrower."[10]

---

[9] "Ethics of Boxing and Manly Sport," by John Boyle O'Reilly: Boston, Ticknor & Co., 1888.

HISTORICAL

Scotland, too, has always been famous for her weight men, not the least of whom was the famous Douglas whose exploits are portrayed in "The Lady of the Lake":

> Indignant then he turned him where
> Their arms the brawny yeomen bare,
> To hurl the massive bar in air.
> When each his utmost strength had shown,
> The Douglas rent an earth-fast stone
> From its deep bed, then heaved it high,
> And sent the fragment through the sky
> A rood beyond the farthest mark;
> And still in Stirling's royal park,
> The gray-haired sires, who know the past,
> To strangers point the Douglas cast,
> And moralize on the decay
> Of Scottish strength in modern day.

And the whole history of English track athletics is most vividly set forth by Mr. Montague Shearman, in his "Athletics and Football," already mentioned, to which volume all who are interested in such matters are hereby referred, while, for the purposes of this chapter, it is perhaps enough for us to note here that modern English track and field athletics date from about the year 1850, that the first Oxford-Cambridge Inter-'Varsity sports were held in 1864, and that two years later, in 1866, the famous London Athletic Club was formed.[11]

Of the history of American track and field Mr. Arthur Ruhl, who is not only himself an athlete, but also a literary artist of unusual distinction, has written most entertainingly in his "Rowing and Track Athletics,"[12] and similar information may be found in the "Book of School and College Sports," of Mr. Ralph Henry Barbour, famous

[10] "How to Become a Weight Thrower," by James S. Mitchel: Spalding's Athletic Library, 1916.

[11] "Athletics and Football," by Montague Shearman. The Badminton Library. London, 1887. And see, also, "Athletic Sports," by H. H. Griffin, Bohn's Library of Sports and Games: London, 1891.

writer of stories for boys. But interesting as all these matters are, once again, since this book is not primarily a history, it is perhaps sufficient for our purposes to observe that American "track" dates practically from the close of the Civil War, that the New York Athletic Club was founded in 1868, and that the Amateur Athletic Union and the Intercollegiate Association both held their first meetings in 1876, since which date the whole history of track and field in America, with some natural ups and downs, has been marked, on the whole, by a steady advance, with a constant increase in popularity and a corresponding improvement in the quality of the records achieved.

Thus, at a glance, we have before us the whole history of these ancient sports, rich in romantic suggestion, dating from the shadowy days before the birth of Homer down to the modern "Olympics," with their great concourse of athletes from many different parts of the world. Surely, to take part in track athletics—perhaps even to add his name to the long list of champions of the past—is a worthy ambition for any boy.

12 "Rowing and Track Athletics," by Samuel Crowther and Arthur Ruhl: The Macmillan Company, 1905.

CHAPTER II

WHY TRACK ATHLETICS ARE POPULAR

THE reasons for the popularity of track athletics may be summarized under two main heads. First of all, there are those reasons which, in greater or less degree, characterize all manly sports—namely, that track and field athletics are a distinct benefit to a man, and a benefit not only physically, but mentally and morally as well.

The physical advantages of exercise are so universally acknowledged at the present day that they need only to be stated to be understood. The athlete abstains from liquor and tobacco. He does not eat unwholesome food. His daily "workouts," followed by bathing and massage, keep his body vigorous and clean. And at the same time his mind is filled with healthy, natural outdoor ideals. He is not growing old too fast in an endeavor to rival the pathetic figure of the London gamin who says, "I'm ten years old, but if yer goes by the things I know, I'm most a hundred."

As for the mental benefits of track and field athletics, I am confident that the public at large does not in the least realize that these sports furnish a great opportunity for the development of brain as well as muscle. To take a concrete example, there is a prevailing and most erroneous impression that throwing the hammer is a game which calls merely for the exercise of brute strength. Yet this is far from being the case. A man who has never seen a hammer before spreads his feet wide apart, swings the missile awkwardly above his head, hands high and elbows bent, and when he attempts to make his throw loses his balance and very often falls at full length, while the hammer is hurled a distance of perhaps forty or fifty feet. - At the other extreme, we find a skilled performer like Ryan, the record holder, turning around three times within the narrow limits of the seven-foot circle and hurling the weight, with perfect control in every particular, some hundred and eighty feet. Between these two extremes lies the long course of training and practice, the gradual discovery of the different points which the athlete must acquire in order to become a successful performer. He must reason out for himself why the hammer is swung in a certain way and why the distribution of the weight of the body and the position of the feet bring about given results. In a word, while weight, strength and physical condition all play their part, their relative importance is slight compared with the knowledge of how the throw should be made. The same rule holds good in all other branches of track and field athletics. It is doing the thing in the right way, the "knack" which counts. It is brain first and muscle next.

Lastly, track and field sports are something more than mere pastimes. True, they are primarily a recreation and a consequent aid to the more far-reaching aims of our daily life, but running through them all there is an undercurrent which calls forth and develops the same characteristics which make or mar us in affairs of greater moment. The athlete learns to appreciate the good qualities brought out in himself and in his mates by actual competition. He learns to value the great quality of gameness, the spirit which fights on undismayed in the face of apparent defeat, and again and again at the last moment pulls out a victory. He learns to respect the rights of his antagonists and comes to realize that his individual success or failure is nothing compared to the success of the meeting in which he is participating, that he must regard the rights of the officials and the spectators, and that true sportsmanship, and not the desire to win at all hazards, is the spirit which should govern competition. Nowhere, to my knowledge, has this last point been better emphasized than by Professor McKenzie, when he says, "The rules and ethics of competition present a constant opportunity to fill the receptive mind of the boy with consideration for a fallen opponent, to give him that frank and modest acceptance of victory or defeat characteristic of the true sportsman who loves the game above the prize and the generous rivalry of the contest rather than victory alone."[1]

Having thus enumerated the advantages which track and field athletics share in common with other sports, there remain to be considered those benefits which belong particularly to running, jumping and throwing the weights. Not only, as we have seen in Chapter I, are these sports the most natural of all exercises, but there is, in addition, something about them which is peculiarly individual; in no other form of competition does a man, both literally and figuratively, "stand on his own feet" to a greater extent than he does in "track"; and this fact is admirably brought out by Mr. Shearman, in his excellent volume on "Athletics and Football."

"All must agree," says Mr. Shearman, "that running, walking, and leaping are the most simple and genuine of all competitions. When a Derby is won it is always a point for argument whether the greater credit is due to the horse or to the jockey; and when Cambridge is badly beaten over the Putney course there is always the critic to say that the Oxford weights were better arranged, that erratic steering threw away the race. or that the losers

[1] Introduction, by Professor R. Tait McKenzie, to Michael C. Murphy's "Athletic Training." New York: Charles Scribner's Sons, 1914.

were underboated. The athlete who wins a big race owes nothing to his apparatus, and his success can only be due to his own excellence or to his opponent's shortcomings. And even if running be more unsociable than rowing, it has the counterbalancing advantage for the individual that his success cannot possibly be ascribed to others. In every eight on the river there is said to be one duffer, and every one of the eight can be certain that some one considers him to be the man. In athletics a "duffer" can only win by the help of a handicap; the cause of his success is then evident, and if he gets the prize he takes little credit with it. When the athlete has got a pair of the best shoes, a zephyr, and a pair of silk or merino drawers (called by courtesy knickerbockers) just *not* coming down to the knee, so as to leave that useful portion of the leg free, he has got all the stock-in-trade required to win half-a-dozen championships. The science of athletics, then, consists in the scientific use of the limbs; the tools of the athlete's trade are the thews and muscles of his own body, which God has made and man cannot refashion."[2]

Moreover, "track" is the most democratic of all our sports, both in the sense that it is free to all, and also in the sense that there are so many different events, calling for so many different varieties of height, weight and temperament, that almost any man has a chance to "make good" in at least one event upon the programme. Upon this point of the democracy of track sports I wrote fifteen years ago. I believed then in the truth of what I said; I believe it even more firmly to-day; and therefore venture to quote the first page of the Introduction to "Practical Track and Field Athletics," without so much as the alteration of a single word, as follows:

[2] "Athletics and Football," by Montague Shearman. The Badminton Library. London, 1887.

WHY TRACK ATHLETICS ARE POPULAR

"The high place which atletic sports and exercises occupy in our national life is a fact not open to argument. While we very properly encourage all branches of athletics and follow with interest the careers and records of those who excel in each particular branch, it is peculiarly in keeping with what the founders of our constitution were wont to term 'the genius of our institutions' that we should bend our best energies toward encouraging sports which are not restricted to a favored few, but are open to the people as a whole.

"Thus it is fitting that track and field sports should occupy an important position in the domain of athletic exercises. Football is confined largely to the Universities and Colleges; baseball consumes a great deal of time, tennis and golf take time and money as well; but track and field athletics, to borrow an expression used by ex-President Cleveland in speaking of the ideal democracy, seem particularly designed to 'give the rank and file a chance.' Sufficient capital to purchase a running suit and a pair of spiked shoes, sufficient nearness to one of the many outdoor athletic fields or indoor gymnasiums and a spare hour somewhere in the course of the day are all that are required to give any one a chance to develop his latent possibilities at some one of the many forms of exercise open to him."[3]

Later writers have expressed similar views. Thus, from the standpoint of the college athlete, Mr. Arthur Ruhl tells us that "The good that has come from track athletics can hardly, I believe, be exaggerated. Other sports may be more exciting to the spectator, and more fun for the man who is in the game; almost any man, I dare say, would rather stroke a winning crew or make a winning touch-

---

[3] "Practical Track and Field Athletics," by John Graham and Ellery H. Clark: New York, Fox, Duffield & Co., 1904.

down than win by a few inches a hundred-yard race. But no other college sport can be indulged in by so many men; no other sport opens such possibilities to the average man and the duffer. And it is the average man and the duffer who need looking after and need encouragement. The man who can make an eleven or a crew doesn't need any physical training. He is either already a 'born' athlete or of a temperament that will get vigorous play and exercise whether or no. The track teams of our colleges and schools have not only drawn into athletics and healthy sport thousands of men who might otherwise have grown up with flaccid limbs and undeveloped lungs, but they have had their social influence as well, and to many a man who might otherwise have remained a hopeless outsider they have given the chance for which every undergraduate rightfully yearns—to do something and be somebody and in some way serve his college."[4]

Similarly, also, Mr. Alfred Shrubb takes up the matter from the point of view of the so-called "average man," and says, *"Mens sana in corpore sano* is the essence of truth. You can look around the world and you will find the most healthful men, the most reasoning men, the greatest leaders, are men who have taken active exercise in some form or other.

"Take Professor Goldwin Smith and he will tell you that he owes his longevity and soundness of mind and body, in his upwards of fourscore years, to horseback riding. The late William Ewart Gladstone had a penchant for chopping down trees. Hon. A. J. Balfour affects golf. And so it goes, all deriving benefit from exercise.

"We cannot all ride horses, chop down trees or play golf. A young man must have considerable wealth before

---

[4] "Rowing and Track Athletics," by Samuel Crowther and Arthur Ruhl: The Macmillan Company, 1905.

he can afford to keep a nag in his stable, own an estate, or meander leisurely for miles each and every day. But he does not need to have a great deal of money to ride a bicycle, to row a boat, to run a race, to put the weight, to walk, to jump, or to throw the hammer, and thus he, as well as the man of wealth, can take his exercise, but in a different way."[5]

In a word, then, track and field athletics are deservedly popular because they furnish an opportunity for the development of brain and muscle, because they teach a man how to conduct himself toward his fellows, and because they are the most natural, the most individual and the most democratic of all our sports.

[5] "Long Distance Running," by Alfred Shrubb. Toronto, The Imperial News Company, 1909.

CHAPTER III

BIBLIOGRAPHY

THE first treatise, in English, on track and field athletics (so far as I am aware) is contained in "British Rural Sports," by "Stonehenge," published by G. Routledge & Co., London and New York, in 1856, in which volume we find hints on training, a description of the various events, and a chapter on the treatment of injuries which may occur in the course of preparation for athletic contests. These hints on training, it is interesting to observe, are remarkably sound, and contain much that could be read to advantage at the present day, as, for example, the author's reference to "The grand principle which every man who values health should constantly keep in view, namely, that no one should attempt to compete in any contest requiring agility or strength, unless he has had such a preparation as shall enable him to perform his task without feeling any ill effects from it." But when we come to specific information as to the various events, the text is less noteworthy, and there is a certain haziness as to times and distances which was apparently quite common at this period. For instance, the world's record for the standing broad jump is twelve feet, one and one-half inches, but "Stonehenge," after describing the "Standing-Leap over a Height," goes on to say that the "Standing-Leap over a width is effected in the same way, but with less contraction of the limbs, and more swinging of the arms. The greatest width I have ever known thus cleared was fourteen feet."

BIBLIOGRAPHY

Another volume published about this same time was "Every Boy's Book." The earlier editions I have never seen, but from the preface to the twelfth edition "Every Boy's Book," Edited by Edmund Routledge and published by George Routledge and Sons, London, 1876, it appears that the first edition appeared in 1855. Here also, as in the volume by "Stonehenge," we find much that is sound and helpful, but the haziness with regard to records is even more pronounced, and there is a quaintness in the style which is irresistible. Bearing in mind that the world's record for 600 yards is 1 minute, 10 four-fifth seconds, for 1,000 yards 2 minutes, 12 two-fifth seconds, and for the running high jump 6 feet, 7 five-sixteenth inches, the following passages cannot fail, I think, to amuse the athlete of to-day. "Running" and "Leaping" are both included under "Gymnastics", and are thus described.

"RUNNING"

"Running is both useful and natural; it favours the development of the chest, dilates the lungs, and, when moderate, is a highly salutary exercise. To run fast and gracefully one should as it were graze the ground with the feet, by keeping the legs as straight as possible whilst moving them forward. During the course the upper part of the body is inclined a little forward, the arms are as it were glued to the sides, and turned in at the point of the hips, the hands shut, and and the nails turned inwards. The faults in running are swinging the arms, raising the legs too high behind, taking too large strides, bending the knees too much, and in not properly managing their wind. In all running exercises the young should begin gradually and never run themselves out of breath at any time. By careful practice a boy may soon acquire the power of running a mile in ten minutes; this is called moderate running: in what is called prompt running a thousand yards in two minutes is thought very good work, and in quick running 600 yards in a minute is considered good."

"LEAPING"

"The High Leap with a Run"

"The leaper should go fairly and straightly over without veering to the side, and descend on the ball of the foot just beyond the toes.

"A good leaper of sixteen years old ought to leap four feet six inches, and an extraordinarily good leaper five feet. Adults well trained will leap six, and some have been known to leap seven feet."

Another most entertaining volume of this period is "A Handbook of Gymnastics and Athletics," by E. G. Ravenstein and John Hulley; London, Trubner & Co., 1867. This book is primarily a treatise on gymnastics, but the incidental references to athletics are really very funny, as when we are informed that "In the High Leap a spring-board should not be permitted," and, with respect to training in general, "A nap after dinner has much to recommend it," and "About half past eleven prepare for bed. You change of course your shirt." In the matter of diet, also, the ideas of the authors were liberal to a fault, as in their reference to "breakfast, consisting of tea or coffee, with stale bread and butter" (causing the reader dreadful doubts as to the quality of the latter article) "a couple of eggs, a chop, chicken, *or anything else you fancy or can afford.*" Surely, those were the kind of broad-minded men under whom it would have been a genuine pleasure to train.

BIBLIOGRAPHY

It is obvious, therefore, that in these early works there is not a great deal which is of value to the close student of track and field athletics, but in 1887 there appears a book of a very different stamp, namely, "Athletics and Football," by Montague Shearman, to which numerous references have already been made in Chapters one and two of the present volume. The merits of this book, which can scarcely be overstated, may briefly be summarized as follows. In the first place, the Chapter on "The History of Athletic Sports in England," is scholarly, complete and remarkably interesting; quite a model of its kind. In the second place, to quote from the Author's Preface, "A word must be added about the illustrations to this volume. Many are engraved from instantaneous photographs, taken by Mr. G. Mitchell, who attended some of the chief football matches and athletic gatherings of the season. The veritable attitude and action of the men have thus been obtained. So far as the author is aware, the present is the first occasion in which the newest development of photography has been utilised for illustrating a work upon athletic sports." And in the third place, again in the words of the author, while he does not "actually go so far as to elaborate an actual manual of training," he does "offer some reflections and reminiscenses" on running, jumping and weight throwing which contain much that is useful, and which, written throughout in a lively and most readable style, furnish a vivid picture of track and field sports in England at the date when the volume was published.

Mr. Shearman's book was followed four years later by Volume V in Bohn's "Handbooks of Athletic Sports," published by George Bell & Sons, London, 1891, the first 120 pages of which are devoted to "Athletics" by Mr. H.H. Griffin. Like Mr. Shearman's books, this work contains some interesting historical information, and much sound practical advice on the proper methods of planning and conducting an athletic meeting. There are also some excellent "special articles" by experts and record holders, on the science of performing the different events, and some good hints on training in general, although it may perhaps fairly be said that on the whole this volume marks no great advance over that of Mr. Shearman.

And now the United States begins to be heard from. In 1888 John Boyle O'Reilly, in his "Ethics of Boxing and Manly Sport," published by Ticknor & Company, of Boston, had made casual references to the history of track athletics, and in 1893 appeared Mr. Walter Camp's "Book of College Sports," published in New York by the Century Company, about fifty pages of which are devoted to "track." Of necessity, therefore, the author's treatment of this subject is somewhat general, yet it is universally recognized that as a writer upon athletics Mr. Camp has "touched nothing which he has not adorned," and these chapters on track and field sports are no exception to the rule.

Next, in 1896, came a book which made another long stride forward in the progress of the literature of track and field; namely, Mr. Herbert Lee's "Track Athletics in Detail," published in New York, by Harper & Brothers. The text of this volume is remarkably good, and may be read to advantage even at the present day, but the point where the author made his name worthy of enduring fame was with regard to the illustrations, for while, as we have seen, Mr. Montague Shearman was the first to appreciate the value of the instantaneous photograph as a means of illustrating the performance of an event, Mr. Lee "went him one better" by perceiving that a *series* of such photographs, taken at various stages, will show the student the form and manner of performance almost as, clearly as if the contestant were standing bodily in front of him, going through the event for his special benefit.

Stated in this bald fashion, this may not sound particulary impressive, but the fact remains that after thirty years' experience upon the athletic field, I am sure that if I were a novice at any given event, obliged to "work out my salvation" for myself, and were given my choice between any number of printed pages, describing the event in minutest detail, or half-a-dozen good "action pictures" of some well known champion, I should unhesitatingly choose the pictures in preference to the text.

Again, Mr. Lee's book was published at a peculiarly fortunate time. The famous international games of 1895 had been held the year before, and we are thus favored with pictures of Wefers, Kilpatrick, Conneff, Sweeney, Hickok and many others, men who, if they could appear at our modern championships in the their form of that date, would give the athletes of to-day all they wanted, and presumably a trifle more, for "furlongs" in 21 and one-fifth seconds, miles under 4.16, half-miles under 1.54, and high jumps of six feet, five and five-eights inches, are not yet being recorded with any alarming frequency.

Eight years after the publication of "Track Athletics in Detail," appeared in the same year, 1904, "Practical Track and Field Athletics," by John Graham and Ellery H. Clark, and Ralph Henry Barbour's "Book of School and College Sports," and, in the following year, "Rowing and Track Athletics," by Samuel Crowther and Arthur Ruhl. These three volumes were published, respectively, by Fox, Duffield & Co., of New York, by Appleton & Company of New York, and by the Macmillan Company.

Of the merits of "Practical Track and Field Athletics," modesty, since I was one of its authors, will not allow me to speak, although it may be permissible to note that it sold steadily for fifteen years, and that, after a careful re-reading, I have not hesitated, in the present volume, to draw freely upon it in the matter both of illustrations and of text.

Mr. Barbour's book, like that of Mr. Camp, does not pretend to be an exhaustive treatise on track and field, but it contains much of value, as does Mr. Ruhl's, and both volumes, written by men of proved ability in the literary field, will well repay a careful reading.

And now, to return to England, the Imperial News Company, of Toronto, published, in 1909, Mr. Alfred Shrubb's excellent treatise on "Long Distance Running and Training," and in 1913 appeared "The Complete Athletic Trainer," by Mr. S.A. Mussabini, written in collaboration with Charles Ranson, and published by Methuen & Co., Ltd., of London. This latter volume is, in many respects, a very remarkable book indeed. The author, to be sure, has a violent prejudice against the "crouching start" for sprinters, and considers that the old standing start is superior, in which belief, I venture to think, he must be quite alone at the present day; but apart from this, the book is a through analysis of style in athletics and is written throughout in such an enthusiastic and philosophical spirit that no man interested in running and walking can afford to let it pass unread.

At about this time, also, a number of additional volumes were published in the United States. "Track Athletics," ten small volumes by Arthur S. Jones, was published in 1912 by Small, Maynard & Co., of Boston, and in 1914 appeared no less than three different books, Michael C. Murphy's "Athletic Training," published in NewYork by Charles Scribner's Sons, "The Book of Athletics," edited by Paul Withington, and published by the Lothrop, Lee & Shepard Company, of Boston, and "Athletics in Theory and Practice," by Ernest Hjertberg, published in New York by G.P. Putnam's Sons. Also, in 1915, appeared a revised edition of R. Tait McKenzie's "Exercise in Education and Medicine" (originally published in 1909: The W. B. Saunders Co., Philadelphia and London), which volume contains a chapter on track athletics, with some excellent illustrations. All of these books, especially, perhaps, those by Mr. Murphy and Mr. Hjertberg, are of undoubted value, are filled, from cover to cover, with sound advice for the athlete, and, added to their list of predecessors, certainly cover most adequately the whole domain of track and field.

Mention should also be made of the series of pamphlets in Spalding's Athletic Library published by the American Sports Publishing Company, of New York. This series includes "How to Become an Athlete," "How to Sprint," "How to Run 100 Yards," "Athletic Training for School Boys," "College Athletics," "Athlete's Guide," "All-Around Athletics," "Distance and Cross-Country Running," "Marathon Running," "How to Become a Weight Thrower," and "Walking for Health and Competition." These pamphlets are noteworthy for the excellent illustrations which they contain, and at least four of them are of genuine importance to the student of track and field, namely, "How to Become an Athlete," by James E. Sullivan, "How to Sprint," by Arthur Duffey, "How to Become a Weight Thrower," by James S. Mitchel, and "Distance and Cross-Country Running," by George W. Orton.

Many special articles, also, have been published in the magazines on various phases of track and field athletics. Among these are the series by Malcolm W. Ford, including "Distance Running," 18 "Outing": 205; "Athletic Training," 19 "Outing": 421; "Specialization in Athletics," 30 "Outing": 574; "All-Around Athletic Championships," 31 "Outing": 81 and "Remarkable Athletic Performances,"

35 "Outing": 603. Of unusual interest, also, is Mr. J. S. Mitchel's "Athletic Giants of the Past," 38 "Outing": 269, and other valuable articles are "By-Gone International Athletic Contests," by W. B. Curtis, 36 "Outing": 350; "What Makes Man a Sprinter," by Paul C. Phillips, 42 "Outing": 230; "Deerfoot, the Indian Runner," 29 "Cur. Lit.," 484: "The Fastest Sprint," by A. Kidd, 40 "Outing": 433; and "The Record Breakers," by T. I. Lee, 25 "Munsey," 472.

CHAPTER IV

TRAINING IN GENERAL

It is a truism that no workman, however skillful, can turn out a piece of perfect workmanship unless he has the proper tools with which to work. Similarly, no matter how much knowledge of his chosen branch of sport a runner or a jumper or a weight thrower may possess, he cannot convert theory into practical results unless he is physically in good trim. This, then (of course after a thorough medical examination to make sure that he is good general condition), is the first problem which confronts the athlete before he comes to the second and, technically, more important one of how to acquire proficiency in any given event. He must try to discover how much exercise, how much sleep, how much food and what kind of food he requires to put himself in the best possible condition.

First of all, it is important to note that within the last half century both theories and methods of training have undergone a radical change; and this contrast between the old days and the new has nowhere been set forth to better advantage than by Mr. James E. Sullivan, in his pamphlet, "How to Become an Athlete." "Thirty-five or forty years ago," says Mr. Sullivan, "the professional trainer prepared a man for competition very much after the fashion a horse was trained. He dieted him, physicked him and worked him almost unceasingly. The athlete had certain hours to sleep, certain hours to work, and certain things to do which tended to make athletics a bore. That system has all been changed. There is no more physicking or dieting, and athletics are run on the basis of 'make the athletes enjoy themselves.'

"Everything tends toward play. The strict training table is practically out of existence to-day. An athlete can eat most anything he wants to, but he must abstain from fatty foods, and things that are indigestible. He must realize that under no circumstances must he use tobacco, or any form of intoxicants. Such must be tabooed as though they were poison. They have no value, absolutely. It cannot be gainsaid that what the average athlete wants most is daily exercise and a proper amount of sleep."

Mr. Sullivan, in the passage just quoted, does not over-state the severity of old-fashioned training methods, which are described both entertainingly and instructively in Chapter VI of Mr. Montague Shearman's "Athletics and Football," while a splendid and inspiring comment on what training really means is furnished by Mr. Arthur Duffey in his "How to Sprint," when he tells us that "Training properly conducted should not be an ordeal to be feared, but, on the contrary, should be a process that brings out all that is best in the athlete and stores up a nerve force of vigor that is more or less completely under the control of the one who trains faithfully and intelligently."

But although, as Mr. Sullivan points out, training to-day is little more than a matter of plain common sense and right living, still there are a number of important general principles which the athlete, and the trainer of athletes, should keep constantly in mind.

For example, if some young athlete should ask for a fixed set of rules by which to govern himself in training, the answer must be that no such rules can be laid down. Probably no two men are exactly alike in temperament and characteristics, so that a trainer with a number of athletes under his care must study each one individually until he is reasonably sure that a certain course of exercise, sleep and diet will bring about certain results. Moreover, the athlete himself soon learns his own capabilities and limitations, and thus Mr. Montague Shearman, in his "Athletics and Football," says, "Every man who has been a couple of seasons 'on the path' should be able to train himself," and similarly Mr. H. C. L. Tindall, (who, by the way, as far back as 1889 ran the 440 in 48½ seconds, and the 600 in 1.12) writing for Mr. H. H. Griffin's "Athletics" in Bohn's "Handbooks of Athletic Sports," states that "Every man must to a large extent be his own trainer. Written laws are all very good in theory, and as a sort of outline for training they are excellent, but each must modify them to suit his own peculiar constitution."

Again, it is probably true that the average athlete is more apt to overtrain than to undertrain. He enjoys his work and is apt to do too much of it, making a possible gain in strength and endurance at an almost certain sacrifice of the feeling of spring and buoyancy which accompanies the very top of physical condition. And when one is overtrained it is not always a mere matter of a few days' rest to put a man right again, but it often means a lay-off for weeks before the athlete recovers his form. It is especially important that on the day of actual competition the athlete should step to the starting line with plenty of energy in reserve, and it is a good plan to cease work altogether or to be content with the very lightest practice for two or three days before an important meeting. Mr. Michael C. Murphy, in his "Athletic Training," advises nothing but light work for an entire week preceding the day of competition, and the results obtained by the teams which have trained under Mr. Murphy's guidance are surely the best possible testimony to the soundness of his ideas.

With regard to the important question of diet, much has been written, and the subject is carefully considered by Mr. Michael C. Murphy in his "Athletic Training" and by Mr. Ernest Hjertberg in his "Athletics in Theory and Practice." The gist of the whole matter is well stated by the Rev. W. Pollock-Hill, champion "miler" and record holder in his day, in an article written for Mr. H. H. Griffin's "Athletics" in Bohn's "Handbooks of Athletic Sports." "The ordinary man," says Mr. Pollock-Hill, "in dieting himself for running need really make very little difference from his ordinary food if he has been accustomed to wholesome and healthy fare." Thus the "bill of fare" should consist, for the most part, of cereals, eggs, light soups, beef, lamb, mutton, steak, chops, chicken, well-cooked vegetables, fruit, light puddings, dry or milk toast, and bread, not too fresh.

A few other rules which are almost self-evident may be noted to advantage. Plenty of sleep is a prime requisite, tobacco and alcohol are strictly prohibited and worry and nervous strain must be avoided if possible. Ice water must not be thought of. Plenty of cool spring water cannot do the slightest harm as long as care is taken not to drink an excessive amount at meal times. A light rubdown before exercising is beneficial and prevents the danger of straining a muscle, especially during the period of Fall training when the days begin to grow colder. A thorough massage after exercising is most beneficial and keeps the muscles from stiffening or growing sore.

Finally, a word should be said as to the effect of athletic training upon the health of the participant. It is a common argument that the strain of a hard race cannot be a good thing for the heart, but careful investigation of the subject by experts tends to show that this danger is imaginary rather than real. Thus, Dr. Woods Hutchinson, in an article on "Athletics and the Heart," in "Outing," volume 56, page 428, says: "There is the soundest of biological reasons why running, or fighting until you drop is seldom fatal, or even permanently injurious. Scarcely one of our male ancestors, human or prehuman, for the past five million years, but has been compelled by the sternest of necessity to pass that form of civil service examination and survive it, not once, but a dozen times. If you couldn't run until you were on the verge of dropping dead, either to catch your dinner, or to avoid becoming something else's dinner, the chances of your days being long in the land were slim and poor."

A spirited defence of a reasonable indulgence in track sports is also to be found in Michael C. Murphy's "Athletic Training," and similar evidence is furnished in an extremely interesting "symposium" on this subject, entitled "Are Track Athletics Harmful to Young Men?" to be found in the "Medical Times" for March, 1916.

It should be observed, however, that after the athlete has once accustomed himself to taking a good deal of exercise, a sudden change to a sedentary life may certainly cause serious results. This point is well brought out by Mr. Murphy, in his above mentioned book, and also by Dr. Hutchinson in an article entitled "The Real Danger of Athletics," in "Outing," volume 57, page 168.

CHAPTER V

TRACK ATHLETICS FOR BOYS

AT WHAT age should a boy "take up" track and field athletics? This, of course, is merely one sub-division of the whole question of a boy's physical development, and the answer to it is that it is largely, after all, a matter of common sense. No one, for example, would dream of taking a boy ten or twelve years old, and training him for a Marathon race; such an act would be so absurd, so indefensible and so contrary to all standards of physical training that the aid of the Society for the Prevention of Cruelty to Children might well be invoked to put a stop to it. And yet, on the other hand, I sometimes think that the same society should be consulted in those cases at the opposite extreme, where well-meaning, but over-cautious parents insist that Willie shall not play with "rough" boys, that he must not soil his clothes and that he must take part in no athletic sports more strenuous than the "safe and sane" game of croquet. In a word, then, the happy medium lies somewhere between these two opposing poles; let the small boy be outdoors as much as possible; let him race around and "play hard," as long as he does not attempt anything obviously beyond his limitations; like all young animals, this is the time when he requires a lot of active exercise and thrives upon it.

With regard, however, to the specific question of track athletics, the boy himself answers that question until he is at least ten or twelve years old. Up to that time, the average youngster's tastes lie in different directions, and his mind and body alike are too much on the move to allow him to take much interest in "correct form" at jumping, running, or throwing anything except stones and snow-balls. But somewhere around the age of thirteen or four-teen the boy will see some important track meet and will at once become fired with enthusiasm to become a champion sprinter, vaulter or weight man. This is the time, not to blunt, but to guide his enthusiasm; to explain to him the scientific basis which underlies all these sports, and to start him practising, not overzealously, but intelligently, so that later on, when he gains added strength and muscular development, he will have already learned the rudiments of these games, and will be in a position to make the most of those physical gifts with which Nature has endowed him. And of course it goes almost without saying that the school or family physician, or both, will examine him from time to time, to make sure that his exercise is doing him good, and not harm.

I am quite aware that there is nothing startlingly novel in these views, but I state them here because, even in these days of comparative enlightenment with regard to the problems of physical education, common-sense rules are frequently broken, and so-called trainers and coaches, taking advantage of a boy's willingness and enthusiasm, seem to forget that he is still immature and undeveloped, and ask him to perform feats which in reality are far beyond his powers. "Make haste slowly"; there is no better rule; and a "symposium" culled from writers of authority upon this subject will, I think, go far toward proving the wisdom of such a course.

"No one," says Herbert Lee, in "Track Athletics in Detail," "ought to begin to train for any athletic event much under the age of sixteen. Until that time few boys are sufficiently developed physically to be able to stand the strain of regular athletic work." "The ideal way," says Michael C. Murphy, in his "Athletic Training," "for boys under sixteen years of age is to 'play at athletics,' and I have never encouraged boys under this age to train for any athletic competition as one generally understands training. I do not mean that a boy under sixteen years of age should not compete in track and field events. Such competition will do him no harm, if he is careful not to run too great a distance or engage in other competition of a severe nature. A boy twelve years old or less should not be allowed to run more than 220 yards, and that not very often."

To the same effect is the advice of Mr. Mussabini, in his "Complete Athletic Trainer," save for the fact that he is even more desirous of "being on the safe side." "Boys and youths under twenty years of age (at the least)" says Mr. Mussabini, "must be content with much less exacting work until they are grown up to manhood. They only need to practise, without exerting themselves severely, to find style and get a grasp of things. The rest will come later on." And, finally, Mr. James E. Sullivan, in his "How to Become An Athlete," states that "From the age of ten to sixteen it is safe to start explaining to the boy how to do things in athletics, but never to train him as the expert is trained," and further, "I have always felt that it is detrimental to the boy's athletic career to have him scientifically trained before he has arrived at the age of eighteen. Prior to that his training should be simply of the play type."

To these safe and conservative views the information should be added that some years ago there was a genuine reaction against the high degree of development which had been reached in interscholastic athletics, and many warning stories were told of "school-boy phenomenons" who ran so fast, and so often, in their school days that they exhausted their vitality and never amounted to anything upon the track when they went to college. In one or two scattered instances, this criticism was deserved; but the only cases in which I ever heard of interscholastic athletes doing too much work and exhausting their vitality were cases of the distance runs; ninety-nine times out of a hundred, the boy who practises conscientiously and intelligently and who makes a name for himself in school athletics will continue to improve after he goes to college and will achieve equal distinction there. There is nothing about jumping or vaulting or throwing the lighter weights, or even about sprinting, that is going to harm the average healthy boy; on the contrary, from rational indulgence in these sports he will derive much pleasure and much benefit as well. As to the quarter mile, the half, and the longer distances, I merely insert a word of caution to the effect that during the growing period, when a boy's heart does not quite keep pace with the rest of his physical development, it is just as well to be on the safe side; there is plenty of time for athletics later on; a good solid foundation of health and strength comes first, and on this the superstructure,—the fun and excitement of competitive athletics may be securely built afterward.

But though it is better to err, if one is going to err, on the side of safety, it must be admitted, in all fairness, that cases of injury from track athletics are very rare indeed. As Doctor Hutchinson has pointed out, in the article quoted in a previous chapter, we have the pleasant knowledge that we have inherited from our remote ancestors a wonderful ability to "stand punishment" and still be able, in the language of the prize ring, "to come back for more." Give the laws of health but half a chance, and the body responds nobly, like the wonderful piece of machinery that it is.

In conclusion, there is one thing which it is often hard for a boy to realize; namely, that no branch of track and field athletics can be mastered off-hand. It simply is not possible; a boy might as well expect to begin the study of the Greek alphabet on Monday and to be reading Homer at sight on Tuesday.

Therefore, let the young athlete learn to curb his impatience; let him read and ponder everything that he can find on the subject of track athletics; let him watch carefully the star performers on track and field, and let him do his own practicing not only regularly but intelligently, not doing things blindly because some one tells him that is the way to do them, but always trying to discover the fundamental principles which govern each event. This is the road to success.

I shall never forget a letter which "Pooch" Donovan, Harvard's famous trainer, received one day from an aspiring young athlete, which read as follows: "Dear Mr. Donovan: There is going to be a set of games in our town next week, and I am very anxious to 'bring home the bacon.' Knowing your reputation as a trainer of athletes, will you kindly send me by return mail full directions for winning the hundred yards dash, the hurdle race and the mile run."

Alas! however, for the young aspirant; this was "too large an order" even for the skill and experience of Mr. Donovan. Champions have been discovered in many strange ways, but I doubt if one ever "brought home the bacon" after one week's training, carried on by the popular methods of the correspondence school.

CHAPTER VI

SPRINTING

American Amateur Record, 100 yards, 9 3-5s.   Dan J.
   Kelley, June 23, 1906; H. P. Drew, March 28, 1914.
   220 yards, 21 1-5s.   B. J. Wefers, May 30, 1896;
   Dan J. Kelly, June 23, 1906; R. C. Craig, May 28,
   1910; May 27, 1911; D. F. Lippincott, May 31,
   1913; H. P. Drew, Feb. 23, 1914; George Parker,
   Oct. 2, 1914.

THE term "sprint" or "dash" is confined to distances
which a man can traverse at top speed and includes any
distance from the ten yards dash sometimes found on the
program of indoor athletic meetings, up to about three
hundred yards.   As Mr. Montague Shearman has well
phrased it, "Sprinting, or sprint-running, is the technical
name given to the running of those short distances over
which a man can spurt or 'sprint' at top speed without a
break.   The rough-and-ready experience of the last gen-
eration, which almost stereotyped the distances and condi-
tions of racing, decided that 300 yards was the limit of
sprinting distance, and that the next distance for racing
purposes—the quarter of a mile—was something *sui
generis*, and distinct from sprinting."[1]   The standard distances, however, which come at once to mind whenever
sprinting is talked of are the one hundred yards dash and
the two hundred and twenty yards dash.

[1] "Athletics and Football," by Montague Shearman.   The Badminton
Library.   London, 1887.

TRACK ATHLETICS UP TO DATE

It is encouraging, at the outset, to observe that a champion sprinter may be of practically any height or weight. On this point all the authorities are agreed. Thus Mr. Walter Camp, in his "Book of College Sports," says: "Tall and short, light and heavy, there are few men who are prevented by physical makeup from competition in one of these dashes. Brooks at 170 pounds, and Myers at 110 pounds, made one of the prettiest 220-yard contests ever seen in America, and both could run a fast 100."[2] And similarly Mr. Shearman, "Certainly your sprinter may be tall or short, may be of any weight up to thirteen stone, though he is rarely a featherweight. He is more often inclined to be fleshy than to be thin, and may be of any height, though he rarely is over six feet." While Malcolm W. Ford cites the case of George Wallace, one of the fastest sprinters of all time, who was five feet ten inches in height and weighed, in condition, one hundred and ninety-six pounds.[3]

Some authorities, however, believe that the configuration of the thigh is a distinguishing characteristic of a great sprinter. On this point Arthur Duffey says: "As a rule, the body should be symmetrical, the limbs long, especially from the thigh to the knee;"[4] and Mr. Mussabini claims that "The greatest determining factor of all is the long thigh, flattish at the sides and bulging out on top and behind. That is the sprinting leg; and it is better if the under leg be short; first, because there is not so much to lift; secondly, because the action is bound to be of the creeping, easy kind; and, thirdly, because the swing of the thigh determines the length and speed of the striding."[5]

---

[2] Walter Camp's "Book of College Sports": New York, The Century Company, 1893.

[3] "Specialization in Athletics": Malcolm W. Ford. 30 "Outing"; 574.

[4] "How to Sprint": Spalding's Athletic library.

[5] "The Complete Athletic Trainer": S. A. Mussabini.

Yet on the other hand it should be noted that Dr. Paul C. Phillips, who averaged the measurements of seventy-four leading sprinters, apparently does not believe in the "length of thigh" theory, and selects a number of other characteristics as more properly typical of the genuine short-distance man.[6]

Entirely apart, however, from the question of a sprinter's build, there is one thing without which he can probably never become a "top-notcher," and that is nervous energy, which Arthur Duffey characterizes as "the foremost requisite of an ideal sprinter."[7] Arthur Ruhl, too, expresses the same idea when he says, "Your sprinter, to be really a fast man, as we reckon speed in these days of better than ever time, must have a certain combination of strength and spring and nervous energy, a dynamic *je ne sais quoi,* which can no more be acquired by training than one can acquire six fingers, or blue eyes, or an extra cubit of stature."[8] And similarly Michael C. Murphy, "It requires a peculiar combination of strength, agility, and nervous energy to make one a successful sprinter, and if nature has not blessed the athlete with these attributes no amount of hard work or coaching can make him a world champion,"[9] and Mr. Mussabini, "The short-distance or sprint-runner stands for the concentrated essence of speed and the acme of vitality. He represents a bundle of compressed energy which expends itself quickly, but in doing so accomplishes the uttermost limits of what the human frame can achieve in the way of locomotion."[10]

[6] "What Makes Man a Sprinter": Paul C. Phillips, M.D. 42 "Outing," 230.

[7] "How to Sprint," by Arthur Duffey. Spalding's Athletic Library.

[8] "Rowing and Track Athletics," by Samuel Crowther and Arthur Ruhl.

[9] "Athletic Training," by Michael C. Murphy.

[10] "The Complete Athletic Trainer," by S. A. Mussabini.

And now, assuming that the athlete has at least a trace of this necessary "pep," we come to a consideration of the art of sprinting itself.

Of the utmost importance, of course, is the proper method of "getting under way." Up to about thirty-five years ago, all sprinters started standing up with their left foot on the starting line and the right foot some distance behind it, according to their length of limb. Gradually, however, that method of starting has become obsolete, and to-day practically every one uses the low or crouching start, which experience has proved, beyond all question, to be the fastest.

How did the crouching start originate? This is a question much easier to ask than to answer with certainty. Mr. John Corbin, in an article entitled "Starting and Starters," in "Outing" for May, 1893, says on this subject, "The precise history of this crouching start would be difficult to write. Its origin is, perhaps, in an old trick by which professionals used to fleece greenhorns. The sharper would make a bet that he could beat his victim in a hundred-yard dash, starting with his body on the ground. When it came to the race, he would make holes for his toes and put his hands on the scratch, letting his body touch the track. His start would then be similar to the modern start, except that he would be stretched out farther behind the scratch, and would have to use his arms in throwing his body upward."

Arthur Duffey, also, considers the problem a hard one to solve, and dismisses it with the remark that "It is very difficult to ascertain who was the first sprinter that introduced this peculiar manner of starting, as many old-time runners claim the distinction."[11]

Mr. Herbert Lee, however, in his "Track Athletics in

[11] "How to Sprint," by Arthur Duffey: Spalding's Athletic Library.

Detail," names Mr. T. I. Lee as the inventor. "Up to within five or six years," he says, (writing in 1896) "the standing start was universal, but in 1889 or 1890 Lee, of the New York Athletic Club, introduced the crouching start, and since then that has become the standard in America." Mr. Ralph Henry Barbour, in his "Book of School and College Sports," published in 1904, also gives to Mr. Lee the credit of being the inventor, adding to Mr. Herbert Lee's testimony "a wealth of corroborative detail." And, most important of all, Mr. T. I. Lee himself, in an article in "Munsey," volume 25 page 472, states definitely that he was the originator of the "crouch."

"It was," says Mr. Lee, "while training—or, rather, limbering up—at Travers Island, one day after some unusually severe racing, in 1889, that we stumbled on the method of starting now in vogue all over the world. Several New York Athletic Club men were practising starts on the soft turf. At that time, all runners started from an upright position. I was the only sprinter in the group, and as a handicap, to make the starts more equal, I crouched on my hands and knees. Then I tried lifting my knees, still crouching, with my head over the mark and hands just behind it. Much to our surprise, we soon discovered that I could start faster than from an upright position. It seemed unaccountable at first, but repeated trials convinced us. I began using the new start in races, and it enabled me to beat men who had previously beaten me. In a few months everybody was using it. Sherrill, of Yale, used a crouching start to keep steady on his mark in 1886, but it was radically different from the present style, in that he kept his knee on the ground."

This last sentence in Mr. Lee's article explains, doubtless, why Mr. John Corbin, in his article on "Starting and Starters," above referred to, says that Sherrill, of Yale, was the first amateur of note to try the crouching start. Mr. Corbin adds that Sherrill never made a great success of it, and this version of the story is adopted by Mr. Arthur Ruhl in "Rowing and Track Athletics." Neither Mr. Corbin nor Mr. Ruhl, however, was apparently aware that "Mike" Murphy was Sherrill's instructor, but this was evidently the case, for Mr. Edward R. Bushnell, in his preface to Mr. Murphy's book, "Athletic Training," says of Mr. Murphy, "That he was particularly skilful with sprinters was best illustrated by his discovery of the crouching start, which was only one example of his inventiveness. He had experimented with it on himself several years before he taught it to Sherrill, of Yale, who first used it in an intercollegiate meet." Moreover, Mr. Murphy himself, in his book, comes out flat-footedly with the statement, "The crouching start was first introduced by me. This was in 1887, at Yale, and Charles H. Sherrill was the athlete who first demonstrated its superiority." And if further evidence were desired, it is furnished by Mr. T. H. Gavin, of Natick, who knew intimately all the famous group of "fliers" which included "Pooch" and "Piper" Donovan, Murphy, Mills, Farrell and others. Mr. Gavin unhesitatingly names Mr. Murphy as the inventor of the "crouch," and states that "Mike" discovered this method of starting, some years before he went as athletic instructor to Yale, hitting upon it almost by accident through his habit of falling forward on his hands, to avoid going over the line, in those days when starting in professional foot races was governed by what seems to us to-day the singularly unsatisfactory method of "mutual consent."

All this seems very clear and decisive, yet we must next observe the testimony of Mr. James E. Sullivan, who was not only a great authority on athletic matters, but who was a firm friend of Mr. Murphy's, and who would surely never have dreamed of trying to take from the latter any credit to which he was entitled. Yet Mr. Sullivan, in his pamphlet, "How to Become an Athlete," says, "The standing upright start which was universal twenty-five years ago is obsolete to-day in sprint races. The 'crouch,' which should be called the 'Kangaroo' or 'Australian' start, is the perfect and up-to-date method of starting.

"This peculiar style of starting, known in America as the 'crouch' start, has been, in recent years, a subject of much discussion as to where it was first used. This man, and that, claimed that he originated the 'crouch.' It is a well known fact that the author of this little handbook took up the question with Mr. Richard Coombes, editor of the 'Sydney Referee' of Australia, because the writer felt that the 'crouch' start came from Australia to America, and then went to England and other European countries. For several years, Mr. Coombes, without doubt one of the greatest experts on athletics in the world conducted a thorough investigation of the 'crouch' start, and it is now admitted that 'Bobby' McDonald, a famous Australian sprinter, was the first athlete to use the 'crouch start.' It is stated that he got the idea from watching the Kangaroo, and for years it was known as the 'Kangaroo start.'"

Without attempting, then, to pass final judgment on the vexed question of the origin of the crouching start, let us proceed to examine the start itself. The athlete begins by measuring a short distance back from the starting line and there digging a hole for his left foot. I use the phrase "a short distance" advisedly, and for two reasons. In the first place, there is no absolutely settled rule; the athlete's length of limb must be taken into consideration. And, in the second place, even when the authorities undertake to lay down a general rule, they are not in entire accord.

PLATE 1.

"On your marks!" T. F. Keane, one of the fastest sprinters ever produced in America.

Three inches behind the line, says James E. Sullivan; four inches, say John Graham and A. S. Jones; five, say Arthur Duffey and J. W. Morton; not more than six, says "Mike" Murphy; six to nine, says Herbert Lee; ten, says Ralph Craig. A good "rough-and-ready" rule, I think, is to place the tips of the fingers on the line, and extend the thumb backward as far as possible, the spot thus reached being the proper place to dig the hole for the left foot.

PLATE 2.

"Get set!"

The skilled performer is not satisfied with making a few scratches in the cinders with his spikes, although the novice often seems to regard this as sufficient preparation. The cinders should be carefully dug up with a small trowel or hoe for a depth of several inches at right angles to the direction in which the sprinter is going to run. The position for the right foot is then found by placing the right knee opposite the middle of the left foot, and the spot

PLATE 3.

"Go!"

where the right toe rests while the right leg is in this position is the place to dig the hole for the right foot. Both
hands are placed on the starting line, with the fingers as
a rule extended and the arms perfectly straight. When
ready to start the right knee is raised from the ground, the
body is moved forward, and the athlete is ready for the
signal. As has been intimated, however, no absolutely
definite rule can be laid down for the beginner as to the
distance of the left foot from the mark and the right foot

PLATE 4.

The first bound.

from the left. He must practice different distances until he feels sure that he has got the best arrangement possible. A change of an inch and a half in the position of the left foot has been known to make a noted sprinter at least a yard faster in the first fifteen yards.

After the starter of the race has allowed the contestants a sufficient time to limber up and dig their holes, he gives the order "Get on your marks," and the athlete assumes the position shown in plate No. 1. Next comes the

Photo by Pictorial News Co.

PLATE 5.

The start of the Intercollegiate Games of 1902 when Arthur F. Duffey, the second figure from the left, made the world's record of 9 3-5 seconds for 100 yards.

command "Set" and the position shown in plate No. 2 is assumed. The weight must be well forward and the mind intent on one thing only, to spring away at top speed at the report of the pistol. With the crouching start there is no excuse for becoming unsteady and starting before the report of the pistol. Sometimes a novice, from excessive nervousness, will start too soon, and as a penalty he

PLATE 6

Halfway down the stretch. Schick of Harvard defeating Moulton of Yale in the dual meet of 1902.

is set back one yard for each offense. Some athletes try to gauge the moment when the starter's finger is curling over the trigger of his pistol and to start just before the pistol is fired, when it is too late for the starter to check his finger. This is called "beating the pistol," and many athletes who would scorn to steal goods or money apparently think that it is perfectly proper to attempt to steal distance from their competitors in this manner. A little reflection, however, will make it evident that trying to "beat the pistol" is nothing less than rank dishonesty, and a man who wins a race by such means can have little upon which to congratulate himself.

The athlete must realize that it is impossible to bound instantly into full stride. The first leap from the mark, in Arthur Duffey's phrase, is "a jabbing motion thrown directly from the hip and kept as close to the ground as possible." Or as Ernest Hjertberg has expressed it, "one must not think about taking any long first tep, but only endeavor to get the foot on the ground again as soon as possible." A series of these short, quick steps must be taken before the sprinter is able to get fairly into his stride.

A very common error in starting is to allow the body to assume an upright position too rapidly. The body should come up gradually, as shown in plates 3 and 4, and correct running position is not usually reached, according to Michael C. Murphy, until the sprinter has covered from twenty to twenty-five yards.

And now, assuming, for the moment, that the athlete is fully under way, let us pause to consider some of the peculiarities of the sprinter's gait, for the days have gone by when the short distance man simply "went out and ran as fast as he could;" the modern youth is of a more inquiring turn of mind, and rightly wishes to know something more of the whys and wherefores of coaching rules.

The best description of the sprinter is, I think, that given by Mr. Mussabini. "Ordinary running," he says, "simply means pulling oneself along on the downward leg and by the arms. All move in this manner excepting the true sprinter, whose form of running is a push of the feet, made right under the body, with all the muscles behind the leg and up the back brought into the effort. The correct sprint-runner is quite an artificial product. He uses his arms differently; and the angle at which his head and body should be pitched, to bring him up on his toes and keep his legs well under him, is not possible to be maintained but for the fastest running."[12]

It is extremely interesting, moreover, to note that there are two distinct styles of sprinting; namely, the "trotting horse" action, on the one hand, and the "low to the ground" style on the other. Neither of these styles can fairly be called superior to the other; it is all a question of a man's build. "Anyone," says Mr. Mussabini, "whose leg is above the ordinary length from the knee to the ankle must come up high, while others who are comparatively short there will keep their feet much closer to the ground." And again, "There are two extremes in the way of sprinting action, either of which may produce, by the process of more or less lengthy culture, extraordinary form. The first of these is the lithe-legged, high-fighting action with knees thrown out in front like an exaggerated copy of a particularly pronounced trotting horse, "throwing them up and out" as the best of his kind will do. There have been very speedy runners, who covered the ground in this showy, eye-taking manner. They are brilliant by comparison with those who simply seem to paddle along with an easy, slinking gait and their feet striking right under them stride by stride. But mere looks do not make the better runner. This low-down-to-the-ground, almost creeping footwork, if not so attractive, has held its own with all other methods. Both extremes present, of course, perfectly natural striding, and bear evidence to the law that no two men are built or run exactly alike."

To the same effect is the testimony of Mr. Arthur Duf-

---

[12] "The Complete Athletic Trainer," by S. A. Mussabini.

fey, one of the world's superlatively great sprinters, although Mr. Duffey, at the time his article was written, apparently did not agree with Mr. Mussabini that this difference in action depends upon diversity of build. "In very few runners," says Mr. Duffey, in his "How to Sprint," "have I seen the same action displayed as in myself, but in time I hope to see this style universally adopted by all desirous of achieving success. In comparing B. J. Wefers, a fellow college man of mine, let me endeavor to distinguish the different types of actions. One must admit that 'Bernie' was the foremost man of his time, but in studying his style of running, it was directly opposed to mine. His running impressed one of a trotting horse, action perfect, and a more beautiful manner of running was never witnessed. How often did the long limbed Mercury himself startle the spectators with his machine-like strides. On the other hand, contrast my close-to-the-ground action, striding directly from the hip, my upper body working similar to a pacing horse and in perfect unison with my limbs. It is not the beautiful action of my predecessor and it has often been wondered how it was possible for me to cover so much ground, but let me assure the reader that my action of striding from the hip, enabled me to cover the same amount of ground, if not more, than the former champion."

Next, it should be noted that the arms are of great service in sprinting, and that the importance of this fact is generally underestimated. When the hands are lifted from the ground at the start the left arm is moved forward and the right back, as shown in plate No. 3, so that arms and legs are working together in unison immediately after leaving the mark. Many novices make the mistake of throwing both arms forward or back, thus preventing arms and legs from working together until after the runner has gone a considerable part of the distance. The arms are used in bent form, but the question of whether they should be moved straight forward and back or across the body is one which merits brief consideration.

At first sight, there would seem to be a square conflict upon this point. Thus, John Graham, in Graham and Clark's "Practical Track and Field Athletics," says that the arms "are moved almost straight forward and back and not across the body," and A. S. Jones, in his "Track Athletics," says that the swinging of the arms forward and back is "probably more effective" than the other method; while, on the other hand, Mr. Mussabini, in his "Complete Athletic Trainer" claims that "the arms should swing across the pit of the stomach," and similarly Arthur Duffey, in his "How to Sprint," observes that "The arms should be swung diagonally across the chest and worked simultaneously with the legs. This cross arm motion I found of valuable assistance to me in many of my races, as it proved a great help to my retaining the bound. Many sprint-runners have adopted the forward and backward arm motion, this is not a bad style to cultivate, but I believe it is inferior to the cross arm swing. Great care should be taken when practising this arm motion that the arms are not swung too far out, for in such a case the swing is of no assistance whatever, as the position of the body is altered. It is a very easy motion of the arms, the muscles of the shoulders and forearm being brought into play."

Again, Mr. Herbert Lee, in his "Track Athletics in Detail," agrees with Mr. Mussabini and Mr. Duffey in stating that "the arms should be swung across the body rather than alongside of it. This gives better form and makes an easier stride." Apparently, however, this seeming conflict is more apparent than real. Mr. Michael C. Murphy, in his "Athletic Training," admits the value of both styles. "The sprinter," he says, "should make good use of his arms, because they can be made to help the legs in their drive by swinging them forward and upward or by a good, hard cross-motion." And Mr. Ernest Hjertberg, in his "Athletics in Theory and Practice," advances the ingenious and reasonable solution that a sprinter's arm motion, like his leg motion, depends wholly upon his size and build. "I shall first endeavor," says Mr. Hjertberg, "to give an account of the style shown by the short runners, such as it ought to be in order to yield the best result.

"If an example is taken from among the many good short runners that we possess and his style carefully studied, we shall find a number of special details of great interest. During the run he works more with his hips. The legs and body are thrown forward, and the hips are moved powerfully, thus getting a long stride. By this means the strides become as long as those taken by a tall runner, and the reason that a short runner can do this is because he has more control over his body and legs than a tall runner has. A tall runner could not recover so rapidly if he were to run from the hips. The action of the arms also differs somewhat from that of a tall runner. All short runners carry their arms during the race more obliquely across the body, but, in spite of this, they can still have full control of the movements of the body.

"Now the tall runner gets his rapidity of movement chiefly by extending his legs as the knee is raised, and by striding out. His manner of carrying his arms is also essentially unlike that used by the shorter runner, for a tall man carries his arms more with a backward and forward motion while he runs, and not quite so low."

Finally, while on the subject of the arms as an aid to the sprinter, there should be noted the remarks of the cele-

SPRINTING

Photo by Leonard Small, Boston "Globe."

PLATE 8.

An "eyelash" finish in the Intercollegiate 100 yards. Smith of Michigan first, Moore of Princeton second, Teschner of Harvard third.

sists of much practice in starting, fast dashes of from twenty to thirty yards, speed work at from seventy-five to one hundred and fifty yards, and jogging or springing up and down the track to develop springiness. Interesting comment on this "bounding" practice will be found in Arthur Duffey's "How to Sprint," and in S. A. Mussabini's "Complete Athletic Trainer," and I should here emphasize the fact that no one who is interested in all the "fine points" of sprinting should allow either of these books to remain unread, since text and illustrations alike, in both volumes, cannot fail to prove of the very greatest service to the man who likes to study sprinting and sprinters.

There seems to be no doubt that the sprinter's body should be bent slightly forward. As Mr. Montague Shearman observes, in "Athletics and Football," "It is obvious that, if the chest be not thrown well forward, the stride must be shortened by the drag which the weight of the trunk will put upon the legs. This, we think, the pedestrian trainers must well know, as nearly all, and even the mediocre, pedestrians 'run low' when sprinting." And, similarly, Mr. J. W. Morton, in his "How to Run 100 Yards," in Spalding's Athletic Library, states that "I was always taught to run low, that is, the body well forward, so that I miss a certain amount of windage and also get my legs out farther and faster."

Before trying any speed work, at the beginning of the day's exercise the sprinter should jog up and down until he is thoroughly warmed up, and should not sit still at any time during his practice. Also, after finishing the distance he is running, he should remember always to slow up gradually; stopping suddenly is one of the worst things a sprinter can do.

If possible it is a good plan to do your work in company with another runner, for, as Mr. Shearman says, "A man should never practise sprinting alone; he becomes sluggish, and can never really tell whether he is doing well or ill," while Arthur Duffey's advice is that "It is to one's advantage to secure some other runner to race with, as it is a wonderful help to have some one alongside of you. This pacer should always be a runner who is acknowledged to be a faster man, and if it is impossible to secure a fast pacer, place a slower man upon a handicap and endeavor to catch him."

It is wise to use corks in the hands. They are commonly

called grips, and are made of cork with a rubber band running through them, which is passed over the back of the hand before going to the start.

With regard to the amount of work to be done while training for the sprints, schedules for both the one hundred and the two twenty yard dashes will be found in Ernest Hjertberg's "Athletics in Theory and Practice," and in James E. Sullivan's "How to Become an Athlete," the schedules in the latter book being laid out by Lawson Robertson. An interesting point as to the best method of running the "220," is emphasized by Michael C. Murphy, in his "Athletic Training," when he states that "The 220-yard man must develop a long, easy stride," and further, that he must realize the "necessity of learning to swing through this race at almost one's best speed for the first 180 yards, without actually trying every step of the way as in the 100-yard dash."

CHAPTER VII

THE QUARTER-MILE RUN

American Amateur Record, 47s., M. W. Long,
October 4, 1900

IN the "good old days" of track athletics, the quarter-mile run was regarded distinctly as a middle distance event; a contest much more closely related to the "880" than to the sprints. The athlete did not even trouble himself to take a crouching start, and was content to run his race in a more or less leisurely manner, keeping sufficient strength in reserve for a vigorous and sensational spurt at the finish. But alas for the comfort of the quarter-miler, those happy times are gone, and the "440" is to-day probably the severest test upon the whole athletic programme, for as "Tom" Burke, one of the world's great quarter men, once said to me, "It's a hard race, because you are trying all the time to achieve an impossibility, to cover your entire distance practically at top speed, something which no man yet has been able to do."

This estimate of the quarter is generally accepted as the true one. In "Practical Track and Field Athletics" John Graham and I said of this distance, "This race is one of the hardest at which the athlete has to compete, for it requires both speed and strength to become a good quarter-mile runner. Although the distance lies midway between the short dashes and the distance runs, it approaches the former much more nearly than the latter, and is practically a sprint all the way." Similarly, Michael

Photo by J. C. Hemment.

PLATE 9.

T. E. Burke defeating M. Long in the quarter-mile at the National Championships of 1897, in 49 seconds.

C. Murphy calls it "the hardest event on the athletic
programme," and says that it is "more like one sustained
sprint every yard of the way;" James E. Sullivan says,
"I think it should be considered as a long-distance sprint;"
George Orton observes that "The quarter partakes both
of the nature of a sprint and a distance, the speed being
the main element," and Arthur Ruhl gives the most
graphic description of all when he tells us that "The quarter mile, although generally spoken of as a 'run,' is really

more properly a sprint. It is run at almost top speed until the last fifty yards, when the runner squeezes his corks and 'finishes on what he's got left.' "

Training for the quarter mile, while on the same plan as training for the shorter distances, naturally calls for more "staying-up" work. The jogging distances must be lengthened and the speed work must be at longer distances than in training for the sprints, and must not be done at quite so fast a rate of speed. While the stride is the most important thing in the quarter mile, and consequently the point on which the athlete should center the greater part of his attention, he must not neglect practice at starting, for while to-day most championship "quarters" are run on long straightaways with one turn, still much racing is also done on oval tracks, with the starting point only a short distance from the first corner. Thus the fastest man in the race, if a slow starter, may easily become "pocketed" in the confusion which results from a large field of runners turning the first corner together at high speed, and may find it impossible to make up later the distance thus lost. And, in any event, practice at starting is worth while, for there is no opportunity to loaf in the "440" as it is run at the present time.

To acquire the proper stride for running a quarter mile the knees should be well raised and the athlete should run on the ball of his foot with the toes pointed straight forward. The body should be bent slightly forward, and the arms should be moved straight forward and back, and not across the body. In Mr. Ernest Hjertberg's "Athletics in Theory and Practice," in his chapter on "Running the 440 yards," the author says:

"In the matter of style one can run with the arms bent at the elbows, and they should be swung backwards and forwards and never be allowed to become stiff. During

THE QUARTER-MILE RUN

PLATE 10.

"Ted" Meredith winning Intercollegiate Quarter-Mile, 1916, in 47 2-5 seconds.

the run the knees should be drawn up somewhat at each step, but not so much as in the 100 and 220 yards. One can also run with the arms down, but forward and not to the rear of the body, the arms swinging back as in shorter distances.

"The runner must keep close to the ground, and with the trunk steady. Many quarter-milers carry the body so that it rises and falls during the race, but this is quite incorrect, as by its means one soon loses control over the body, and thereby loses speed."

As regards the ideal build for a quarter miler, the comment by George W. Orton, in his "Distance and Cross Country Running" is of great value. "The kind of men," says Mr. Orton, "best suited for the quarter mile are those that have speed, in the first place, and a certain amount of stay. Our best quarter milers have generally been men of about 5 feet 10 or 11 inches in height, sturdily built, and with a long easy stride. Such a man was Maxey Long, the greatest quarter miler that ever lived. Many other fine quarter milers have been built on the same lines.

"There is another type of quarter miler which is almost as common; men on the Myers or Burke style. They were tall and thin. They had plenty of speed and the very length of their stride made up for the lack of stay which would have been fatal in a shorter striding quarter-miler. It is rarely that we see a small man a first-class quarter-miler, but Reidpath and Robinson are both small though very stoutly built. The first class mentioned are the best built for the work, for they combine speed and stay in the most favorable ratio for getting the results."

With regard to the amount of work to be done in training for the quarter, schedules, (not, of course, intended to lay down hard and fast rules) may be found in Graham and Clark's "Practical Track and Field Athletics," and in Ernest Hjertberg's "Athletics in Theory and Practice." George Orton, in his "Distance and Cross Country Running," makes the following extremely sensible observations on this matter.

"It is always a dangerous matter to reduce training to a definite point, for the simple reason that what is one man's meat is another's poison. For this reason, I hesitate to prescribe any daily routine of work. But for the benefit of those who have no trainer to look after their peculiar wants and needs, I shall give the following as a schedule of training for a week.

Monday.—1. Several short sprints away from the mark. 2. Run through the quarter, starting as fast as in a race, and then striking a long, swinging gait. Carry this pace all the way to the tape, but not so fast as to be distressed.

Tuesday.—1. Sprints as on Monday. 2. A 60-yard dash. 3. Run 300 yards, starting out at your best speed the first 40 yards; then settle into a long, swinging gait at quarter-mile racing speed. This will give you the pace without punishing you.

Wednesday.—1. Sprints as usual. 2. Go through 200 yards at a fast gait, paying special attention to stride. 3. If not tired, run a very easy quarter.

Thursday.—Do the same work as on Tuesday, omitting the 60-yard dash if not in fine fettle, that is, if not feeling in running humor.

Friday.—1. Sprints as usual. 2. Go all the way through the quarter trying to develop the long, fast, ground-covering gait that is so necessary for quarter-mile running. Do not sprint at the finish, and do not run so fast as to be distressed.

Saturday.—1. Limber up. 2. Go the quarter at racing speed.

To which schedule Mr. Orton very wisely adds, "Many things may make the above schedule unfitting for certain athletes. The man training for stay should do longer work than is mentioned, while the stayer should do more sprint work than is given. Bad weather may interfere. My rule is to do my long distance work on rainy days. It is dangerous to sprint on a soft track."

＃ CHAPTER VIII

THE HALF-MILE RUN

American Amateur Record, 1m. 52 1-5s., J. E. Meredith,
May 13, 1916

WITH the change from the quarter to the half-mile run,
speed becomes of much less importance and endurance
becomes an absolute necessity. Of course a good half-
miler, a man who can beat two minutes, must be possessed
of a fair amount of speed, but endurance. must be cultivated at all hazards. As George W. Orton puts it in his
"Distance and Cross Country Running," "The event is
still one in which speed plays a part, though it is not so
important as in the quarter. In that event, a man must
be a fine sprinter to go the distance in championship form.
This is not necessary for the half, but more stay is required. Here the athlete must have the latter quality or
he will peter out the last 80 yards and finish in poor time."
It is of the utmost importance that strict attention should
be paid to good form and to the manner of striding. The
knees should be carried fairly high and the athlete should
run on the ball of his foot. Some men acquire the bad
habit of curving the instep, which breaks and shortens the
stride. While a long stride is desirable, the runner must
be careful not to acquire an exaggerated style. The stride
must be natural and comfortable, and he must be able to
sprint when called upon, for, again to quote from Mr.
Orton, "The gait of the first quarter should be maintained
until the last 220 yards is reached, when it is a case of try-

Photo by Pictorial News Co.

PLATE 11.

E. Hollister of Harvard leading his field in the half-mile in the dual games between Harvard and Yale.

ing to get further up on the toes for the sprint home. It is often very difficult to get up on the toes when one has run the first 660 yards at racing speed, but a conscious effort must be made to do it, as, if accomplished, the muscles are acting at different angles and parts that have not been at tension are put to work and the athlete seems to gain a new lease of life."

The body, in running the half mile, should be carried slightly forward, and the arms should not be swung too high, but should be carried, as Michael C. Murphy says in his "Athletic Training," "not in any particular manner, but easily and naturally."

Photo courtesy American Sports Publishing Co.

PLATE 12.

J. E. ("TED") MEREDITH.

Holder of the world's record for the 440 yards (47 2-5s.) and 880 yards run (1m. 52 1-5s.); holder of intercollegiate (University of Pennsylvania) and A. A. U. records for the same distances; winner 800 meters run, Olympic Games, Stockholm, 1912.

THE HALF-MILE RUN

Many tentative schedules of the amount of work to be done in training for the "880" have been complied by different authors. These may be found in Graham and Clark's "Practical Track and Field Athletics," in Ernest Hjertberg's "Athletics in Theory and Practice," in James E. Sullivan's "How to Become an Athlete," (schedule made out by Lawson Robertson) and in George W. Orton's "Distance and Cross Country Running." The real gist of the matter, however, is aptly summed up by Michael C. Murphy, in his "Athletic Training," when he says, "Generally speaking, a good week's training will consist of two jogs at about four-fifths speed for 1,000 yards or three-quarters of a mile, with two fast 660-yard runs at the best speed on alternate days and a trial or race on the fifth day. If the athlete desires to compete in a race at the end of the week he will wish to hold the day before the contest open for very light work, or none at all, according to his condition."

CHAPTER IX

THE MILE RUN

American Amateur Record, 4m. 12 3-5s.   N. S. Taber,
July 16, 1915

FIFTEEN years ago, in Graham and Clark's "Practical
Track and Field Athletics," John Graham wrote of the
mile run that "It is one of the hardest running events on
the entire programme, and the necessary endurance cannot be cultivated in a week or a month, or as a general rule
in a year. Cross-country running is the best work that a
mile runner can do to lay a thorough foundation for the
subsequent training necessary for the mile. No one can expect to do wonders the first season, and as a rule the third
year is better than the second and the fourth better than the
third."

This was sound advice, and that it has stood the test
of time iss witnessed by the fact that ten years later
Michael C. Murphy, in his "Athletic Training," confirms
what Mr. Graham said by stating that "if there is any event
on the athletic programme which challenges the quarter
mile in demanding unusual powers of endurance it is the
mile run. . . . The best kind of training for the mile run
is cross-country running taken in the fall and winter. Endurance is of great importance in this race, and there is
nothing like this kind of work to make any youngster
strong."

It is of prime importance for the beginner to develop
an easy manner of running, for in a hard race like the mile

THE MILE RUN

Photo by Leonard Small, Boston "Globe."

PLATE 13.

John Paul Jones, of Cornell, defeating Norman Taber, of Brown, in the mile run at the Intercollegiates. Later, Taber established a new record for the mile.

an easy style is bound to be of assistance. Every muscle must do its share and all the weight must not be thrown on the legs. The knees do not need to be lifted as high as in the shorter runs, but the stride adopted must be smooth, even, and springy. The longer the stride the greater the advantage to the runner, but he must remember not to over-stride in his attempt to gain ground and thus acquire an exaggerated style. As in the shorter runs, he must run on the ball of his foot with the body carried a trifle forward and the arms swinging easily at the sides.

TRACK ATHLETICS UP TO DATE

A splendid volume dealing with the mile and the other distance runs is the pamphlet in Spalding's Athletic Library, entitled "Distance and Cross-Country Running," written by that great runner and great authority upon running, George W. Orton. Both the text and the pictures illustrate perfectly the correct theory of distance running, and I venture to quote here three passages which I believe contain the whole sum and substance of the matter for the athlete who wishes to excel at the mile.

"The athlete," says Mr. Orton, "should run naturally, thus allowing his muscles to get the reflex action which makes the athlete's task so much the easier and better. The muscles should not therefore be kept at high tension, but be allowed freedom of action. It is this tendency to run stiffly and artificially which has ruined many a promising runner. 'Do not tie up,' was one of the most frequent calls which the late Mike Murphy gave to his men when training."

"Together with ease of gait—and in fact a part of it —is a runner's ability to run fast without 'tieing up,' as they say. The muscles should not be kept at tension except at the end of the race, when they will naturally tighten up under the severe strain laid upon them. Everything should move freely and with a natural reflex action. Many runners have the proper leg motion, but their arms and bodies are kept at tension from the very start of the race. This not only quickly tires the muscles, but it retards the action of the lungs and, to a less extent, of the heart. This is diametrically opposed to the principles of running which, to a great extent, depends upon the rhythm of action that is maintained between the legs, arms and so on of the runner on the one hand and the heart and lungs on the other."

"Mile runners have often discussed the best way to run the distance. Of course, every one has his own special

Copyright Underwood & Underwood.

PLATE 14.

Norman Taber, record holder for the mile run.

ideas, but they all seem agreed that when in shape, the first quarter should be run fast, say somewhere close to a minute. By doing this the miler makes the most of his natural speed. He should then keep up the gait, so that on reaching the half he is getting rather tired. Somewhere during the third quarter, or it may be near the beginning of

L'A—Seventy-eight

the last quarter, he will strike the place where he is about willing to cry quits. But he must then fight off his exhaustion and summon all his strength for the final effort. If on his last quarter, he can change his gait, get up on his toes and sprint, using his hip muscles to their full extent, he will find that he can work up a very good spurt. Conneff once stated to me very briefly the way in which he ran the mile: 'I go the first quarter on my speed,' said he; by the time I reach the half I am getting quite weary; at the three quarter pole I feel dead to the world, but I go another quarter because I have to and because I make myself do it."

It must, then, be evident by this time that no man is going to succeed at the mile unless he is willing to take much pains with his training. "I have always been a great believer in plenty of work for distance runners," says Michael C. Murphy in his "Athletic Training." The following schedule, therefore, is about right for an average week's work: Monday, a mile with a fairly good three quarters and the last quarter easy. Tuesday, a half mile in about two minutes and ten seconds, a rest, and then another easier half mile, sprinting the last hundred yards. Wednesday, jogging up and down the straightaway rather quicker than if running a mile, followed by an easy one and one-half miles. Thursday, a fast half, followed by a rest and an easy three-quarters. Friday, an easy mile, sprinting the last hundred yards. Saturday, a mile trial on time.

When John Graham and I wrote "Practical Track and Field Athletics," in 1904, the idea of a runner's changing his gait on the last lap of a mile so as to relieve the leg muscles by placing a different tension upon them was something of a novelty, and I remember that we advanced this suggestion with considerable diffidence. Experience, however, has proved that the theory is sound; Orton recommends it strongly; and Michael C. Murphy, in his "Athletic Training," (although he happens, at the time, to be speaking specifically of the two mile instead of the mile,) says, "I have always made it a point to train all my distance runners in speed work, independently of training them to develope endurance. Sprinting brings into play a different set of muscles, and when one is tired at the end of seven laps with the long stride of the two miles, if he is any sprinter at all he will be surprised at the easy manner in which he can sprint for a good part of the last lap."

CHAPTER X

DISTANCE, CROSS COUNTRY AND MARATHON RUNNING

LONGER distances than the mile are frequently found upon the athletic programme—for example, the two, three, five and ten mile runs. The method of training for distances, however, is practically the sam in training for the mile, with the the longer the distance and the gr

CHAPTER XI

The One Hundred and Twenty Yards High Hurdles.
American Amateur Record, 14 3-5s. Robert Simpson, May 27, 1916; June 3, 1916.

THE high hurdle race is one of the prettiest and most interesting events of an athletic meeting. There are ten hurdles, three feet and six inches in height, and these are placed ten yards apart, leaving fifteen yards from the start to the first hurdle and fifteen yards from the last hurdle to the finish line. At all well-regulated meetings each competitor has a separate set of hurdles.

Twenty years ago, there was but one style of clearing the hurdles, namely, to curl the leading leg in such a manner that from the knee down it would be almost parallel with the top of the hurdle. But the whole theory and practice of high hurdling was, so to speak, changed overnight when the wonderful Alvin C. Kraenzlein appeared at the Intercollegiate Championships of 1898. Kraenzlein conceived the idea that the hurdler should curl the leading leg only slightly, and in fact should practically stride across the hurdle, and from the moment when he put his theories into practice and completely demolished all existing records both for the high hurdles and the low, the prior method was forever doomed to oblivion.

It is quite true that the old style of hurdling was extremely pretty and graceful to watch, yet it possessed the disadvantage that there was a distinct, even if slight, pause as the athlete cleared each hurdle—a moment when the body lost its highest forward speed, and hung fractionally

PLATE 15.
The old style of clearing the high hurdles. Ellery H. Clark.

suspended in the air. This, of course, meant just so much lost time, and the advantages of the new method are graphically described by Mr. Mussabini in his "Complete Athletic Trainer," when he says, "Nowadays the first-class man seems just to split himself out like a pair of scissors opening, and get astride his hurdles like a passing flash of color, and be down and off for a next performance in the twinkling of an eye. He is all movement and dash, and there seems to be no dead point about his progress any-where."

HIGH HURDLES

Copyright by Underwood & Underwood.

PLATE 16.

Robert Simpson, the record holder for the high hurdles.

A very important point in high hurdling is to make sure of reaching the first hurdle at top speed, for it is in this first fifteen yards that sufficient momentum must be developed to carry a man through the full distance. If he loses here, he is sure to be slow all through, and Mr. C. F. Daft, a former champion and record holder, writing for Mr. H. H. Griffin's "Athletics," in Bohn's "Handbooks of Athletic Sports," gives sound advice when he says, "Go off at full speed, and get over the first hurdle as soon as possible. A great many men make a mistake at this point by taking it too easily for the initial run on the flat, and therefore losing ground, which it is difficult to make up again."

The start used is the same as the sprinting start, but the strides to the first hurdle must be arranged so that the athlete is not too far away from the hurdle or too close to it on his take-off step. Very often it is necessary to shorten the first few strides, or to start with the right foot forward instead of the left, to insure getting this distance correctly. There should be three strides between hurdles after landing. In practice it should be the main object to get as close to the hurdle as possible without touching it, the rear leg coming over with the foot turned outwards and not downwards, since by trailing downwards the toes are liable to pull over the hurdle. It is of the utmost importance to remember that the longer the body is allowed to remain in the air while going over the hurdles the more time is wasted. The correct theory of hurdle racing is to keep close to the hurdles and to the ground, and to bring the legs down again as quickly as possible as each successive hurdle is cleared.

Of extreme importance, also, is the position of the body as the athlete clears the hurdle. If, for example, he should keep his body bolt upright on leaving the ground, the throwing forward of his left leg as he rises to the hurdle will tend to force his body still further back, and he will land on the opposite side of the hurdle in an awkward and "sprawled out" posture, so that he will actually have to wait until he regains his balance before he is able to get under way again. To obviate this, the body must be bent forward as the athlete leaves the ground, a feature of correct hurdling especially noticeable in the work of the famous Robert Simpson, and which is excellently described by Mr. A. F. Copeland, in "How to Become an Athlete."

"For the high hurdle," says Mr. Copeland, "it is neces-

PLATE 17.
Good form over the hurdles. Erdman winning.

sary that the front leg, the first leg over the obstacle, should be as nearly straight out as possible, with the rear leg drawn up as near to right angles as can be done, and tucked up under the body immediately the leap is made.

"There must be another movement in unison with the above while crossing the stick which will warrant the upper body being thrown forward so that the chest nearly lies on the front thigh. This guarantees the quick dropping of the front leg in combination with the pulling of the rear, which makes for a quick recovery and instant readiness for the striding to the next hurdle."

The high hurdler should practise assiduously at starting and sprinting, but should remember that hurdling is hard upon the leg muscles, and should not run through the full distance more than once a week. Daily practice over three hurdles, and some work over six or seven, together with his sprinting work, will give him·all the stamina he needs.

A word, perhaps, should be added as to a very recent development in high hurdling, namely, the position of the arms as the athlete clears the hurdle. Formerly it was conceived that the arms should be extended on either side, as a natural balance, and there are first-class hurdlers who use this style at the present day. Another group, however, are experimenting with an arm action which is more forward and less to the sides, and, in theory, certainly, it would seem that this method has much to commend it, as it emphasizes the sound fundamental idea of getting straight ahead without the slightest fractional check or pause.

CHAPTER XII

The Two Hundred and Twenty Yards Low Hurdles,
American Amateur Record, 23 3-5s. A. C. Kraenz-
lein, May 28, 1898; J. I. Wendell, May 31, 1913;
Robert Simpson, May 27, 1916.

IN this event, as in the preceding, ten hurdles are used,
but they are only two feet and six inches in height and are
placed twenty yards apart, leaving twenty yards from the
start to the first hurdle and the same distance from the
last hurdle to the finish. The lessened height of the hurdles makes the race rather more a question of sprinting
ability and less a question of ability to take the hurdles
properly, although there is a certain rhythm in striding
over the hurdles which at first is not easy to acquire.

The beginner will find that he will be obliged to take
about nine strides between the hurdles, but after some practice he will be able to reduce this number to eight. This
necessitates taking off from each leg alternately, and consequently is a good deal of a handicap, and the best method,
which depends to a large extent upon the athlete's height
and length of limb, is to reduce the number of strides between the hurdles to seven. The best method of taking
the hurdles is that originated by Kraenzlein, namely, to
take them in one's stride with the front leg straight and
without any break or stop in taking off or landing. The
actual clearing of the hurdles is naturally a much easier
task than getting over the "high timbers," and consequently
the athlete does not have to use so much forward action
of the body, nor does he have to use quite the same action

in getting his rear leg over. As Michael C. Murphy puts it in his "Athletic Training," "The lateral stride of the back foot is missing."

As in the high hurdles, the athlete must remember that taking the hurdles high is so much wasted time. He must skim the hurdles as closely as possible, and must not keep his body in the air an instant longer than is necessary.

Training for the low hurdles is on the same plan as in preparing for the high hurdles, but of course "stay" becomes of great importance, and besides practice in starting and sprinting, the athlete should take plenty of the same kind of work that he would need if preparing for a two hundred and twenty yards dash on the flat, and not only this, but should include, also, some of the quarter-miler's training, in order to make sure of acquiring the necessary stamina for the distance. He should do his actual hurdling over from three to six or seven hurdles, in practice, and should run a trial once a week.

With regard to the action of the arms, it is interesting to observe that some of the fastest of the modern champions are tending, as in the high hurdles, to more of a straight forward action, and are doing away with the old lateral action altogether.

CHAPTER XIII

The Four Hundred and Forty Yards Hurdles. American
Amateur Record, 54 3-5s. William H. Meanix,
July 16, 1915.

THE quarter-mile hurdle race was added to the American championship programme in 1914, and it is surely an event which will tax the strength and agility of any athlete in the world. The quarter mile on the flat is bad enough, but when the runner is asked, in addition, to clear ten three-foot hurdles, placed forty yards apart, it almost seems like a case of "adding insult to injury." Many a man who has made a name for himself over the two hundred and twenty yards low hurdles, has determined to "take a try" at the longer distance, and has gone through with flying colors up to about the seventh hurdle, when, in racing parlance, he has suddenly found himself, "dead to the world," and actually unable to negotiate the remainder of the distance. And, in addition to the strength required, it must be remembered that the race is run around a curve, and that there can be none of the nice mechanical precision as to the number of strides between hurdles which is such a help in the two shorter hurdle races. In the quarter mile, the athlete figures his leap over the hurdles by a sort of instinct, beginning either to "chop" or lengthen his stride when he is about fifteen yards away from each successive barrier.

Absolutely the first requisite, however, for this race is "stay." When Mr. Meanix established his record, he went through a long and arduous preparation, in the pre-

PLATE 18.

W. H. Meanix making record of 54 3-5 seconds.

liminary stages of which he trained for three weeks on a
"Miler's" schedule, doing a great deal of "staying-up"
work, and sometimes jogging as far as three miles.   Then,
with this foundation to build on, he gradually shortened
and quickened his work, until on the day of his trial he
was in perfect condition for the test.   As Mr. Meanix expresses it, "A man must have speed—that is, he should
be at least a ten and two-fifths man for the hundred, and

in addition to that, he should not only be able to run a quarter on the flat in about fifty seconds, but should be able to go through a half in the neighborhood of two minutes. And of course, besides these qualifications, he must be a good performer over the hurdles as well, for the three-foot hurdle is too high to stride over as you would take a low hurdle; it requires the form of the high hurdler; and even at that, the last two or three hurdles loom up like six-foot fences as the athlete, despite himself, begins to tire and to lose both speed and spring."

This testimony, from an expert and a champion, will doubtless, then, convince the beginner that the four hundred and forty yards hurdle race is an event which must be taken seriously. On a small scale, it is actually an "all-around" event, requiring great stamina, good speed and a knowledge of the art of taking the hurdles in good form.

CHAPTER XIV

THE RUNNING HIGH JUMP

American Amateur Record, 6 ft. 7 5-16 in., E. Beeson,
May 2, 1914

THE running high jump is one of those deceptive events
which is by no means "as easy as it looks," and much study
and practice is necessary before the athlete really acquires
the proper knack of clearing the bar.

At the very outset, also, it must be admitted that a man
cannot hope to become a really first-class high jumper unless he possesses a certain amount of natural spring, a matter which is well explained by Mr. Montague Shearman,
in his "Athletics and Football," when he says, "The muscles used for the spring are those in front of the thigh
which pass down to the knee-cap. The knee is bent when
preparing for the spring, the muscles are contracted, and
from the sudden and violent straightening of the leg with
a jerk, the impetus is given. A high-jumper, therefore,
must have these muscles not only strong but naturally
springy and elastic, and from this it follows that in a
certain sense the high-jumper, like the sprinter, is born,
not made; for though muscles can be hardened and
strengthened by practice, nothing but nature can make
them elastic. As a matter of fact the high-jumper is
nearly always short-thighed, with a well-shaped knee, a
rather long leg from knee to ankle, and with an ankle,
like the knee, cleanly and delicately shaped."

Assuming, therefore, that the athlete is possessed of at

THE RUNNING HIGH JUMP

Photo by Pictorial News Co.

PLATE 19.

The running high jump. Old style. Mr. Green of Baltimore.

least a normal amount of spring, the next problem for him to master is the proper method of clearing the bar. First of all, he must decide upon the length of his run, and nine times out of ten the inexperienced jumper makes this run too long. There is, of course, no absolutely fixed rule; some men do better with a run of sixty or seventy feet; others start only twenty-five, or even twenty feet from the bar. But for the average jumper about forty feet from the bar is a good distance from which to begin his run, and this forty feet is roughly divided into three parts:

first, a few short steps, merely to gain momentum, then four or five strides at moderate speed, and lastly, three strides into which the jumper puts practically all his strength and energy, though still reserving a little something for the last step of all, which gives him his final impetus as he leaves the ground. As Mr. T. Jennings, former President of the Cambridge University Athletic Club, says, in an article written for Mr. H. H. Griffin's "Athletics" in Bohn's "Library of Athletic Sports," "In high jumping, beginners as a rule make the great mistake of running too hard at their jump. A good high jumper will trust to the last three strides to get up sufficient pace." Or, as the whole theory of the jump was once aptly described to me by the late William E. Quinn, a wonderful performer and a close student of athletics, "The jumper must keep his feet near the ground during his run, for the high jump, properly speaking, isn't a jump at all, but a *jolt.*" And this is absolutely true. The jumper does not so much run at the bar as he comes creeping or sneaking up to it, counting on the concentration of energy in the last few strides to "jolt" him forcibly off the ground.

The idea of the run, with its gradually increasing momentum, once firmly fixed in his mind, the athlete must next turn his attention to the proper method of getting his body over the bar. Thirty years ago, everyone jumped the same way, using what was known as the "side jump" or "scissors jump." As the name implies, the athlete approached the bar from the side, from the right if he jumped from his left foot, from the left if he was a right-footed jumper. As he neared the bar (assuming that he jumped from his left foot), he would throw his right leg high into the air and then draw his left leg up after it, so that an instantaneous photograph of the jumper in the act of clearing the bar would make him look as if he were

Copyright by Underwood & Underwood.

PLATE 20.

Loomis of the Chicago A. C.

sitting upon it. This method of describing the jump
serves to expose its real weakness, for when the bar was
raised to any considerable height, this was precisely what
the jumper did—he sat down upon the bar. Fling his legs
as high as he might, there was no method of getting his

hips out of the way, and he would thus land upon the bar and displace it.

Old traditions, however, are hard to overcome, and unsatisfactory as this method of jumping now appears to us, no one thought of trying to improve upon it until the advent of the famous W. Byrd Page, who revolutionized the whole art of high jumping, and incidentally established a record of six feet and four inches, which was to stand for many years to come. Page, instead of approaching the bar from the side, ran straight at it, and when he left the ground brought his legs straight up in front of him, at the same time turning on his side so that he shot over the bar parallel to the ground, and with legs and body extended in one straight line, like an arrow leaving the bow.

The advantages of this style are obvious. In the first place, by clearing the bar in a horizontal instead of in a perpendicular position, the jumper is spared the tremendous effort of lifting the weight of his body straight upward into the air; and in the second place, he retains far greater control over the muscles of his body and instead of displacing the bar with his hips, he is able to arch or wriggle them over the bar in safety. It is no wonder, then, that the superiority of Page's style was immediately recognized, and with various modifications by later jumpers, it is the style which is still in vogue at the present day.

This method of going over the bar with the body parallel to the ground has been variously described by different writers. "In high jumping," says Michael C. Murphy in his "Athletic Training," "the object is to throw the entire body up to and above the normal level of the head and then to get the body across the bar without touching it." "The body," observes James E. Sullivan, in "How to Become an Athlete," "should clear the bar in a wiggle, snake-like, and not stiff nor bolt-upright." And similarly Arthur

Copyright Underwood & Underwood.

PLATE 21.

C. Larson clearing 6 feet, 5 5-8 inches.

Ruhl, in "Rowing and Track Athletics," tells us that "So far as any upward motion is concerned, his head is almost as stationary as though it were hinged to an imaginary point and the body were a rod, which was flung upward and over the bar."

The one fundamental fact, then, for the athlete to remember is that he must not adopt the old side jump, with body perpendicular and hips in a position where, at any considerable height, they are bound to displace the bar, but that he must run straight at the bar, and at the moment when he leaves the ground his mental picture of what he is trying to accomplish should be that of a man flinging himself *bodily* into the air. It is not enough merely to lift the legs, but the whole body, hips, waist, arms, legs, all must work in unison to attain the greatest possible height. The best rule I ever had given me was that of a former champion who said: "Imagine that you see before you not merely a slender bar to be cleared, but a solid shelf or piece of board extending parallel to the ground, and that you are trying to throw your whole body into the air so that you will slide along that shelf, flat on your side."

There are, at the present day, two principal styles of correct high jumping. First, there is the plain "tuck up your legs and shoot over" style, used by Alma Richards and many other good men. This style has the merit of simplicity, for the jump is merely one tremendous bound, with the body held rigid as it shoots over the bar. I am confident, however, that a still better style is that known as the "wriggle." This was the jump used by the famous Michael F. Sweeney, and it is the jump used to-day by Wesley Oler and other jumpers of superlative excellence. The principle of the "wriggle" is as follows: instead of making one motion in his jump—upward and forward at the same time, as in the "shoot" style—the jumper, in the "wriggle" style, divides his jump into two distinct parts. First, as he leaves the ground, he devotes all his energies to throwing himself straight up into the air, getting his "layout" at the same time, and it is clear that by applying all his strength to this one end, he can get higher in the air than if he were expending an equal amount of effort in shooting upward and forward at the same time. It is also clear, however, that the jump must lack the forward drive of the "shoot" style, and that unless the jumper makes some further effort, he will fall upon the bar from lack of momentum. Here is precisely where the "wriggle" comes in, for at the moment when the athlete feels himself in danger of striking the bar, he makes, with back and hips, a distinct throw or twist of his body (which after a time becomes perfectly involuntary) and thus arches or "wriggles" himself over the bar. This style, it is true, is complicated, and therefore harder to learn than the "shoot" style, but it is a much more scientific and highly developed method of clearing the bar. Most high jumpers to-day who use this style jump a trifle from one side or the other, and get the hip which is nearest the bar out of the way by means of this throw of the body, but there was nothing of this sort in the jumping of the great Michael F. Sweeney, of whom it may be said, without fear of exaggeration, that he attained absolute perfection of form. Sweeney went over, practically back to the bar, and an excellent description of his form at his greatest heights (the text accompanying a splendid picture) is given by Mr. Herbert Lee in his "Track Athletics in Detail." "Thus," says Mr. Lee, "although up to six feet Sweeney clears the bar in an upright position, when it comes to a higher leap he springs as high as he can from the ground, and then heaves his torso and shoots his legs forward, twisting his body in the air until he comes into the position shown in the picture. He has to depend entirely upon the momentum of his run and the mid-air twist on top of the bar to get his shoulders and head over."

Mention should also be made of the peculiar style of clearing the bar usually described as the "California" jump. Here the athlete runs at the bar from the side, but the jump itself in no way resembles the old side jump, or, in fact, any of the other styles which we have been considering, for in these other jumps the athlete clears the bar with his hips nearest it, while in this Western style the athlete half dives, half rolls over the bar so that in the act of clearing it he is practically stomach down and hips up. This method possesses one noteworthy advantage: in all the other jumps there is a stopping of momentum as the athlete leaves the ground; even in the "shoot" style the weight of the body is thrown backward; while in this Western jump there is no diminution of momentum, but a continuous forward motion until the ground is reached. On the other hand, many people object to this style on the ground that the jumper, as he descends, has an opportunity to hold the bar on with his arm, and thus in many cases obtains credit for a height which he did not really clear. These objectors (and personally I am inclined to agree with them) think that this style should be barred as a trick jump, which is not a fair test of an athlete's real ability as a jumper. Incidentally, it is interesting to note that while this style of jumping is supposed to be of very recent origin, there is a picture in Mr. H. H. Griffin's "Athletics," in Bohn's "Handbooks of Athletic Sports," which volume was published in 1891, which shows a high jumper clearing the bar apparently in the same fashion as that used in the "California" jump. The picture is entitled, "The gymnastic-roll-over," and the author's comment on it is "effective, but not elegant."

A word, in conclusion, as to the best method of practising. The besetting sin of all novices is to wish to go ahead too fast; therefore the beginner must make a point of practising with the bar at a low height, a height where he need not worry as to whether or not he is going to clear it, and may accordingly think only of jumping in good form. When he is conscious that he is getting a good lift from the ground, and a good "layout" as he clears the bar, he may then venture on greater heights. After he becomes reasonably proficient, it is a good plan to have a regular "tryout" once a week, in order to discover what height he can really clear. But most athletes are apt to jump too much rather than too little, and to practise three times a week is enough for anyone.

CHAPTER XV

THE RUNNING BROAD JUMP

American Amateur Record, 24 ft. 7 1-4 in., M. Prinstein,
April 28, 1900

A SUCCESSFUL broad jumper must possess two qualities, speed and spring. As James E. Sullivan observes in "How to Become an Athlete," "The most essential thing in broad jumping is speed and ability to hit the take-off in proper stride, and then be able to throw yourself in the air, so as to get out the greatest distance. The athlete who can retain his speed, hit the take-off and shoot high in the air, draw his legs well up under him until he is about ready to strike the ground, when he must shoot them out forward, land in the pit and throw himself forward, makes a good broad jumper. Like everything else in athletics, exhaustive practice is necessary for perfection."

As far, then, as the question of speed is concerned, the athlete should remember that practice in sprinting is a very important part of his training, and he should do a good deal of fast work at the short distances, keeping well up on his toes, and not forgetting to make good use of his arms and shoulders as well as his legs. But at the same time he should also bear in mind that speed is not to be emphasized at the expense of spring, for, as a matter of fact, it does not require any very great skill to run down for the take-off at full speed, and almost any sprinter of fair ability can clear nineteen or twenty feet without effort. The successful broad jumper, however, is the man who

THE RUNNING BROAD JUMP

PLATE 22.

The running broad jump. Ellery H. Clark leaving the take-off.

realizes that it is a genuine jump which he is attempting and not merely a sprint with a perfunctory lifting of the legs at its conclusion.

The first thing for the beginner to do is to find out the exact length of the run which he must take preparatory to the jump itself. Generally speaking, it is customary to take a run of about ninety feet, and to cover this distance in about sixteen strides. Let the athlete, then, make two marks, one about fifty feet from the take-off, the other about forty feet back of that. Let him start from this

Photo by Pictorial News Co.

PLATE 23.
Meyer Prinstein, in mid-air.

first mark, and run down toward the nearer mark at fair
speed, striking it with the foot from which he intends to
make his jump. From this point on, he must run at top
speed, but without any thought of jumping or of altering
his stride to strike the board; on the contrary, he should
run with strides of natural length as if the board were not
there at all, stationing a friend at the take-off to see
whether his eight strides bring him short of the board or
over it. If, for example, his last stride brings him three
feet short of the board, let him alter his nearer mark to

THE RUNNING BROAD JUMP

Copyright Underwood & Underwood.

PLATE 24.

C. E. Johnson, of Michigan, one of America's best broad jumpers.

forty-seven feet; if he comes, on the other hand, a foot and
a half over the board, let him lengthen his run to fifty-one
feet and six inches. Thus, after considerable practice, he
will eventually find that he has fixed upon a mark from
which he may run at top speed, without worrying over his
ability to strike squarely upon the take-off.

It should be noted, however, that there is no hard and
fast rule which governs the method of the run down to the
take-off. Some athletes prefer to have only one mark,
about seventy feet from the board, and to sprint from that

mark at full speed. Again, Michael C. Murphy, in his "Athletic Training," while advising a long run, considers that the last six strides, covering a distance of from thirty-five to forty feet, are where the final intense effort should be put forth; and Ernest Hjertberg, in his "Athletics in Theory and Practice," advocates still another plan. "The way to form the run," says Mr. Hjertberg, "is to place a mark about seven yards from the outside edge of the board. A second mark is put about seventeen yards away and, finally, a third at about twenty-seven yards, care being taken that the foot with which the jump is to be made is placed on the twenty-seven yards mark. From this mark up to the seventeen yards mark the speed should be pretty fast. Between this second mark and the seven yards one, the speed should be as great as possible. The same speed is kept up for the remainder of the distance, letting the legs run loosely, but drawing the body together somewhat and shortening the last two strides, so as to gather strength, even at this highest speed, to be able to throw the body upwards.

This last point as to not getting "spread out" on the last stride is an important one. As George W. Orton observes in his "Athletic Training for School Boys," "The last stride previous to the take-off should be a short one. This will allow the jumper to gather himself together, get his jumping leg well under him and to get a powerful leg drive. In other words, it will give his jumping muscles full play.

There now remains to be considered the matter of the jump itself. And first of all, let the beginner realize that the running broad jump *is* a jump, and that it is not enough to sprint for the take-off, lift the knees, and go skimming through the air close to the ground, without attaining elevation. Elevation is essential. We found, in discussing the high jump, that it was not sufficient merely to lift the legs, but that the jumper must fling himself bodily into the air; and the same rule holds true in the broad jump; the athlete must lift his hips, as well as his knees, high into the air.

One other caution is necessary. Almost all beginners are inclined to let the weight of their bodies fall back too soon; as they leave the take-off they throw their legs out in front of them, and this causes the body to tip back, so that it acts as a drag upon the jumper. A golden rule in broad jumping is not to be too eager to get your feet far in front of you at the beginning of your jump. In other words, *don't jump too soon;* keep moving forward as long as possible. It is not until the end of the jump, when gravitation begins to exert its irresistible force, that the athlete needs to think of getting his feet out ahead of him; if he has made a good jump, with his weight well forward, this final fling of the feet is a perfectly instinctive movement, performed without conscious thought upon his part.

In conclusion, the athlete must remember that the broad jump is an extremely taxing event, and that it is the easiest thing in the world to overtrain at it. The best way is to practise plenty of sprinting, and to do quite a little easy jumping, with a short run of twenty or thirty feet, merely to become accustomed to getting well up in the air, without trying for distance. Actual hard jumping, however, should be limited to twice, or, at most, three times a week, and not more than six or eight jumps should be taken in any one day.

CHAPTER XVI

THE POLE VAULT

American Amateur Record, 13 ft. 2 1-4 in., M. S. Wright,
June 8, 1912

As AN object of interest to the spectators the pole vault often suffers from the great amount of time which it consumes, and from the fact that it is usually placed at the very end of the program of events. On the other hand, it is the most spectacular of all the field events and the sight of the athlete clearing the bar at a height in the vicinity of thirteen feet never fails to arouse the enthusiasm of the onlookers.

Just as the hurdle races were revolutionized by the discovery of the straight leg action, so the pole vault, in recent years, has undergone a complete change through the introduction of the shifting of the lower hand upon the pole. In the old days, the athlete grasped his pole with his upper hand slightly higher than the height of the bar, placed his lower hand about three feet below, ran down for the take-off exactly as in the running broad jump, and half sprang, half pulled himself over the bar without altering the position of his hands upon the pole. A glance at plate No. 25 will make clear the disadvantages of this mode of vaulting, for it is impossible to exert any very forcible pull while the hands are placed in this manner. The present method is to shift the lower hand upwards when the pole is placed in the ground so that both hands are close together on the pole. Thus the athlete is in the proper position for

THE POLE VAULT

PLATE 25.
Pole vaulting. The old style.

making a strong effort, and, after he has taken advantage of the natural swing-up which the pole affords him, he pulls up with his arms, gets his feet higher than his head for a clean shoot over, and when the pole is nearly upright lets go, lifts his arms, and arches his body over the bar. It is obvious, therefore, that the pole vault is a great all-around developer; a man needs good speed for his run, and this practice helps his legs, while a strong body and especially good shoulder muscles are a necessity for clearing the great heights.

Courtesy of Boston Herald.

PLATE 26.
The new style: McLanahan of Yale.

Another important, and most beneficial change, in the pole vault has been the introduction of the bamboo pole, which has done away with the great danger of injury from a broken pole, always a menace in former times.

The beginner must realize that he is not going to master the art of pole vaulting in a day, or in many days. Described upon paper, it does not sound difficult, but in practice a long and arduous apprenticeship must be undergone before the athlete really acquires good form. The best article I have ever read on pole vaulting is the one written by Mr. J. B. Camp, for Paul Withington's "Book of Athletics." Mr. Camp was a first-class performer at the vault, and, in addition to this, was a close student of form in athletics. The novice at the vault will do well to read and study with diligence the following extracts from Mr. Camp's essay on the fine art of vaulting with the pole.

"Of the two distinct styles of vaulting," says Mr. Camp, "the most elementary is the easiest beginning for a novice. This consists in not shifting the hands from the position they hold when running down to the take-off.

"Although many coaches as well as candidates neglect it, the exercise of vaulting without shifting the lower hand is the most valuable of all practice stunts. Both novice and expert should practice this way regularly, as here described. It is taken for granted that every one vaults off his left foot, holding the pole on the right side when running. It is best to be content with a six-foot height at first, and have a regular practice mark of 35 to 40 feet from the hole. Hold the pole low, at arm's length on the right side, gripping tightly with the hands about thirty inches apart and thumbs toward the upper end of pole. In the last two strides swing the pole out ahead from the side and let it slide along the ground into the socket, and quickly swing the arms over the head in a wide upward curve. Very little energy or speed need go into the run, as the whole thing is the swing up under the pole. On springing, shove down into and against the pole as if to bend it double. While the lower arm shoves desperately and the upper or right is braced for a pull, the body lifts itself against this fulcrum so that the chest grazes the pole, and the thighs, closely doubled up, slide along it. The muscles connecting the shoulders and torso are the ones which do the work, and they alone have license to tire soon. A full lift without any twist whatsoever will turn the back up and the belly down over the bar, when the handstand on the pole is completed. In the last minute lift with back and arms into a close jack-knife, with the knees near the chin and the cross-bar in between, and shove off clear. In this exercise, as in all other practice work and vaulting at low heights, the standards should be set a foot or more back from the hole in order to give distance as well as height and to encourage a very long swing and a delayed but sharp pull-up. This is in the nature of advance preparation for the greater heights."

After the novice has acquired the knack of clearing the bar in this manner, Mr. Camp then advises his taking the next step and advancing to "Vaulting with a shift, but without a turn and not using a cross-bar. Use the regular practice mark of 35 to 40 feet and, at first, a hold of only as high as you can reach on the pole, when it is standing upright in the hole. Run down slowly, and as you are planting the pole in the hole, slide the lower or left hand up close to the right, and extend the pole high above the head before the jumping foot springs off the ground. Swing out at arm's length until nearing the ground and then pull your head up as far as you can along the pole, at the same time clamping this to the stomach and the knees to the chest. Strike the dirt in this position, where you will hit first on your feet, but overbalanced forward.

"The twin of this may be practised without pit or run, when holding about seven feet up the pole. Plant the pole ahead of you, take a step, and pull up on it until head, knees and hands are together and the pole is passing by the hips, and stay there until it has swung on and dropped you, still hunched up, on your feet. The same thing can be done on a climbing pole in a gymnasium, where the German horse and tumbling are also recommended for vaulters."

THE POLE VAULT

PLATE 27.
The new style. A clean, vigorous vault.

And finally, after all this practice work, Mr. Camp gives directions for the complete vault, as follows: "The marks for the run are the same as for the broad-jump, and measured from the hole where the pole lodges. The jumping foot should take-off from a spot exactly under the hands when they are held at the proper point on the pole for the following vault, the pole being in the hole and the arms extended above the head. On every vault watch the mark your foot makes in the dust and test it to see if it is just under your hands as they hold the pole up high. The manner of holding the bamboo for the run is rather important. The hands grasp it loosely, about three feet apart, so that the forward end is pointing up at an angle of thirty degrees. The body must face squarely down the path; the shoulders alone are twisted toward the line of the pole. The right arm is twisted so that the elbow is directly above the pole. This rests against the heel of the palm, fingers loose. The left shoulder reaches as far forward and to the left as it can go, in order that this elbow may be directly under the pole, which rests between the bent-back first finger and thumb on the palm of the hand. In this fashion one runs practically free of the pole, which balances itself between the palms of the hands. Only the shoulders are askew and the body faces directly forward with no sidewise strain. About three strides from the take-off the pole must be cast ahead spear-fashion, with one hand, and wait in the hole, where it is already swinging up as you take the last stride. As you spring the pole should already be at arm's length, overhead. Failing in this perfection of detail, be sure to shove it up above you as far and as quickly as possible. Don't forget that the whole weight of your body must come against and be sustained by the jumping leg as much as in the broad jump, or your dead weight against the pole will slow its swing quite hopelessly. To this end the run is down in a crouch, in the last few strides, and one has turned off some of his speed and is coasting while gathering strength for the extra effort of the spring."

There is one point of great importance in making a correct vault which often gives trouble to the novice, namely, that the athlete must not hurry his vault unduly, but must take advantage of the natural swing that he gets from the pole. Thus Michael C. Murphy, in his "Athletic Training," says, "The vaulter should let the pole swing him over the bar just as a man would jump a fence by placing his hands on the top rail." And similarly Ernest Hjertberg, in his "Athletics in Theory and Practice," states that "It must be observed that in the pole jump the body is not jerked up, but all the movements must be characterized more by a swinging motion. The body is swung up, and then by degrees it is drawn up by means of the arms. Consequently, it is incorrect to make a too powerful swing, as what is needed here in the spring is to give the body a strong swing which will contribute most to get the extremities up." And the late William E. Quinn used to say constantly to his pupils, "Let the pole carry you up; don't be afraid to trust to your pole."

A wonderful set of photographs, which illustrate the correct method of vaulting better than any amount of description in words, will be found in "Athletic Training for School Boys," edited by George W. Orton, in Spalding's Athletic Library.

CHAPTER XVII

PUTTING THE SIXTEEN-POUND SHOT

American Amateur Record, 51 ft., Ralph Rose, Aug. 21, 1909

PERHAPS no other athletic event furnishes such a diversity of styles as those seen in putting the sixteen-pound shot. Really first-class athletes who have attained proficiency in shot putting differ as to the best method of holding the shot, the position of the hand and arm, the balance of the body and the position of the feet. If the reader doubts this, let him look at the picture of Hickok in Herbert Lee's "Track Athletics in Detail," then at the pictures of Horgan and Rose in Ernest Hjertberg's "Track Athletics in Theory and Practice," and finally at the splendid photographs of Pat McDonald in James S. Mitchel's "How to Become a Weight Thrower." It may, however, fairly be said that much of this apparent difference of opinion depends on the physical characteristics of the performers. A man with a large hand may prefer to hold the shot in an entirely different manner from that employed by a man with a small hand; a very muscular man may prefer a slower style of putting while a light, active man may have to acquire greater speed to make up for his deficiency in weight.

There are a number of cardinal principles, however, on which all students of shot putting are agreed.

First of all, to quote Mr. Montague Shearman, in his "Athletics and Football," "The main point to learn in

PUTTING THE SIXTEEN-POUND SHOT

Photo by Leonard Small, Boston "Globe."
PLATE 26.
The start of the put. Whitney of Dartmouth.

weight-putting is to 'get one's weight on'—to use a rowing
phrase—that is to say, to employ mere arm-work as little
as possible, and to get the impetus for propulsion from a
rapid spring and turn of the body." Other authorities
emphasize this same idea in slightly different language.
"If you watch the men of to-day," says Mr. James E. Sullivan, in his "How to Become an Athlete," "in their at-

Photo by **Pictorial News Co.**

PLATE 29.

Midway in the put. Richard Sheldon of Yale.

tempts to put the shot, you will see them get well crouched
and get the drive from the right leg and the shove from
the body that does the trick. In other words, if you have
not the drive from the body back of your shot, you will
never be able to put the shot a very great distance." The
testimony of Mr. James S. Mitchel is to the same effect.
"All the time," says Mr. Mitchel, in his "How to Become
a Weight-Thrower," "he should never lose sight of the
fact that the motive power for making the weight travel
is created by a rapid spring and half turn of the body;

that the arm work should be employed only in the final part of the effort." And similarly Mr. Ernest Hjertberg, in his "Track Athletics in Theory and Practice," tells us that "the best throw is that given when one feels that the power comes from the legs and travels up along the side of the body and right out to the tips of the fingers," while Mr. Joseph Horner, in an article written for Mr. Paul Withington's "Book of Athletics," states that "from this crouching position the body should spring upward with just enough of a spiral to throw the whole weight of the body behind the right shoulder, moving in an upward and outward direction. During this spiral spring the right arm should be thrust up and out and the left arm should be brought down with force to aid the spiral."

In the second place, the position of the body and of the feet at the conclusion of the preliminary "hop" are of the utmost importance. Equally good performers may adopt different positions at the start of the put, but however this may be, it really makes no vital difference whether the body is faced to the right or left, whether the shot is held close to the body or away from it, or whether it is held in advance of the shoulder or resting upon it. It is the position on landing from the "hop" that is of prime importance in shot putting, and this position does not admit of much variation. The knees are bent, the weight of the body is well forward, and the right shoulder and elbow are lowered in order to get the full weight of the body behind the put. The remarkable series of photographs of Pat McDonald, in James S. Mitchel's "How to Become a Weight Thrower," perfectly illustrate the whole theory of the put, from beginning to end.

In the third place the finish of the put is the time when the chief effort must be made. It is the besetting sin of most novices to start by making a long hop at great speed and to finish with a weak half turn of the body and without any "follow through" to speak of. It is perfectly true that this preliminary hop must not be made too slowly —as McDonald himself says, "It should be a good lively swing, not too fast nor too slow," but as the famous George Gray once said to me, "the athlete must remember that the hop, after all, is only a preparatory movement to place the body in correct position for putting and at the same time have it in motion and not at a complete standstill."

The novice should begin by practising putting from a stand, feet fairly close together, shot held near the shoulder, muscles not tense but relaxed and the elbow held close to the side. A sudden spring is made from the right foot, while the left foot is drawn back with equal rapidity and the right arm, with the full weight of the body behind it, shoots out to its fullest extent. But let the athlete, to quote the words of Mr. Mitchel, "remember to swing his body well around to the front before he starts to shoot out his arm, as it is more important to bring the heave of the shoulder into play than the speed with which the arm straightens out. All the time he should put in an upward direction; or the arm when extended to its full length, after the shot has left, should make an angle of about 45 degrees with the body."

After the performer becomes familiar with this style of putting, he should try the regulation style of putting with a hop. Mr. McDonald, in his article in "How to Become a Weight Thrower," gives an excellent description of the start for this method of putting. "When the athlete begins to take the full measure of the circle he should stand at the back, directly in line with the direction in which he wants to put. He should set himself well, and all the time he should hold the shot in his left hand and

PUTTING THE SIXTEEN-POUND SHOT

Photo courtesy American Sports Publishing Co.
PAT McDONALD.

Position of the body and legs as he jumps to center of circle.

Photo courtesy American Sports Publishing Co.

PUTTING THE SHOT.
A remarkable photo of Martin J. Sheridan.
Showing Martin in a perfect balance after delivery.

until he is ready for the hop, when the shot should be passed to the right hand. There should be the least delay after the ball has been set in the right hand, for if allowed to remain there too long the arm will tire."

It is also important to note the manner in which the so-called "hop" is made, for it is not really a "hop," as the word is generally understood, but is "really more like a shuffle," as James E. Sullivan expresses it in his "How to Become an Athlete." As George W. Orton, in "Athletic Training for School Boys," describes it, "The athlete should glide across the circle," or, as Mr. McDonald himself says, "He should partly scrape his foot along the ground to the center of the circle."

Probably, however, the most important point of all in shot putting is to remember that there must be no pause in the put after landing from the "hop." Many an athlete who has achieved fine form in the rest of his putting has "fallen down" on this particular part of the event; that is, he will make his "hop," then pause perceptibly to adjust the weight of his body for the final effort, and then go through with the put, thus defeating the very object of the "hop," which is to give the body just so much more momentum. This momentum once lost midway in the put, the athlete is doing little more than putting the shot from a stand. Let him remember, then, above all else, that as he makes the "hop," he must at the same time automatically adjust the weight and position of his body so that on the instant of landing he is enabled to spring into the final reverse of the feet and body, and thus achieve a smooth and continuous put, with no "break" between the "hop" and the final thrust.

The beginner at shot putting can stand a lot of work; especially if he can manage to practise at intervals, doing a little work twice, or even three times, in a day. But after he has once got into good shape, and is at the top of his form, then, as Mr. McDonald says, "Half a dozen puts a day will give sufficient exercise. He should learn to get the best there is in him in six puts, for this is the limit of competition. It is rather a poor plan for an athlete to require a dozen puts before he can get his best, when in the competition he is allowed only three in the preliminary trials. That is one of the reasons why most men do better in practice than in the contest. They never learn to do their best in a few tries."

CHAPTER XVIII

THROWING THE SIXTEEN-POUND HAMMER

American Amateur Record, 189 ft. 6 1-2 in., P. Ryan, Aug. 17, 1913

THE gradual evolution of the hammer from the iron head and stiff wooden handle of old times to the brass ball and slender wire handle of to-day has been accompanied by a no less remarkable change in the method of throwing it. The old style, in vogue for many years, was to hurl the missile from a stand, but within comparatively recent years this manner of throwing has been superseded, first by the single, then by the double, and finally by the triple turn.

The athlete, however, must realize that no event on the whole athletic programme is more complicated, or harder to learn, than throwing the hammer, so that he must banish from his mind, temporarily, at least, all thought of throwing with a triple turn, and must make up his mind to begin modestly by learning to throw from a stand.

He should take up his position, standing easily and naturally, with no rigidity of the muscles, with his back turned squarely to the direction in which he intends to throw, and with his feet about eighteen inches apart. The hammer head rests on the ground to the right, the athlete's arms are extended, and his body is turned slightly to the right as the throw is begun. Perfect form for the start of the throw is shown in plate 32.

There are a number of fundamental principles in making the throw which the athlete must take pains to master

PLATE 32.
The start of the throw. J. S. Mitchell.

at the beginning of his training; otherwise he will soon fall into bad habits which it will cost him much time and pains, later on, to overcome. First of all, then, the speed with which the hammer is swung is an important consideration, and must be carefully regulated. It is a constant temptation, not only to the novice but to the more experienced performer as well, to imagine that the rapid swing of the hammer means a powerful throw, but nothing could be more erroneous. Whatever quick work is necessary is done primarily with the body, legs and arms, and the motion imparted to the hammer itself is comparatively slow. In throwing from a stand the weight is swung very slowly the first time, a little faster the second, and the crucial moment is reached midway in the third and final swing of the hammer around the head. Here, as the hammer falls over the right shoulder, every ounce of strength is applied, and the performer pivots around on his left foot, bringing the arms well up and through to give the necessary elevation.

In the second place, the head of the hammer should be kept close to the ground, for if it is swung high in the air, the necessary elevation which marks all good throws becomes a physical impossibility, the hammer flying off on a straight line when it is released. Thus the performer should remember to keep his hands low and somewhat back of him at the completion of each swing, which will result in keeping the hammer head near the ground at a point behind the right shoulder. Also, the arms must not be contracted, and the muscles of both arms and shoulders absolutely *must* be relaxed, to get the free, loose swing which is so hard for the novice to acquire. Mr. Herbert Lee, in his "Track Athletics in Detail," put this whole matter in a nutshell, over twenty years ago, when he wrote, "When the hammer is thrown around the head it should be kept as far as possible from the body; the arms should not be bent nor the muscles tightened, and the shoulders should be allowed to move as easily as possible." And the same idea is also very well put by Mr. James S. Mitchel, in his "How to Become a Weight Thrower," when he says, "In swinging the hammer over the head, the arms should be held as straight out from the body as possible, so that the hammer handle and arms will resemble one and the same connecting rod with the body. As the hammer travels round the body, as much freedom as pos-

PLATE 33.
Correct form in throwing with single turn. Ellery H. Clark.

sible should be given the shoulders and the hands should swing well behind the head, thereby describing as large a circle as possible in the air. The secret of this is that considerable momentum is imparted to the flying ball with very little loss of vital force."

Another very important principle in throwing the hammer is the method of balancing the body. If the body is kept perfectly erect, the pull of the hammer, as it comes back over the right shoulder, throws the body to the right, so that when the hammer is to be delivered, the final effort, instead of imparting the necessary impetus to the hammer, throws the performer completely off his balance. In common athletic parlance, instead of the man throwing the hammer, the hammer throws the man. To counteract this pull of the hammer, the weight of the body is thrown to the left as the swing is begun, bringing the weight of the body on the left leg, while the shoulders, however, are turned toward the right, so that the hammer is kept well back and under good control. Plate 33 shows good form in throwing the hammer, and illustrates the various points which have just been described.

After the beginner has reached a reasonable degree of proficiency in throwing from a stand, the next step is to try throwing with a turn. James S. Mitchel, in his "How to Become a Weight Thrower," expresses his belief that even the novice, when he begins to throw with a turn, should try the double turn at once and not bother with the single turn at all. Personally, I believe that the single turn should be mastered first, and Michael C. Murphy, in his "Athletic Training," agrees with my views. Therefore, it seems at least permissible to describe this method of throwing the weight.

The left foot is the pivot upon which the body revolves and it is preferable to start with it somewhat behind the right, as shown in plate 33. The hammer is then swung twice around the head, exactly as in throwing from a stand, and, on the third swing, the body revolves on the left foot as rapidly as possible. Even greater care than in throwing from a stand must be taken to preserve the proper balance of the body, and to keep the hammer well behind the shoulders and under control. The right foot leaves the ground completely and strikes again in the rear of the left. Then the left foot is brought back and strikes the ground so that the position is the same as in throwing from a stand. Lastly, the final turn is given to the body and the momentum

PLATE 34.
John Flanagan, in the double turn.

thus acquired should mean an added gain of nearly forty feet over the distance attained in throwing from a stand. The finish of the throw is shown in plate 35.

The idea of the single turn once mastered, the athlete should lose no time in proceeding to try the double, for as Mr. Mitchel truly says in his "How to Become a Weight Thrower," "No man ever sent the hammer as far with one turn as with two; that is, provided he had the proper plan of executing the double turn." And Mr. Mitchel again speaks truth when he adds, "Not a few have tried three turns with seeming success, but there is not such an advantage between three turns and two turns as between one and two; and, anyway, two turns inside the seven-foot circle without a foul generally taxes the activity of the most agile." Therefore it seems certain that a man should feel that he has really mastered the double turn before he tries the triple, which is difficult enough to test the strength and agility of the best man who ever wore a shoe.

Mr. Mitchel, in the passage just quoted, speaks of the "proper plan of executing the double turn." What is this plan, then, and how does throwing with a "double" differ from throwing with a "single" turn? The answer is a simple one, but before stating it, I should like to say a word, at this point, regarding Mr. Mitchel's pamphlet. "How to Become a Weight Thrower," is, I am confident, the best thing of its kind ever written, and its author has scored a genuine success. The pictures of Ryan, McDonald and McGrath are absolutely faultless, and no higher compliment could be paid to the text than to say that it measures up to the standard of the illustrations. Mr. Mitchel's little book is the "last word" on weight throwing, and should be read and re-read by all who are interested in this subject.

And next, to return, after this brief digression, to the difference between the single and double turns. For one thing, in throwing with the double turn, the left foot is not placed behind the right, but both feet are almost on a line. This, however, is comparatively a minor detail; the real point of difference is as follows. In the single turn, the hammer is kept *behind* the body; that is the prime secret of that method of throwing; but to throw a "double" or "triple" in such a fashion, and keep inside the circle is an impossibility; as the late William E. Quinn once said of

PLATE 35.
The finish of the throw. Ellery H. Clark.

such an attempt, "that is something the devil himself couldn't do." Therefore, the secret of the "double" and "triple" is to let the hammer come well around *in front* of you, and trust to your speed in turning to, so to speak, "catch up" with it, and have it behind you when the final heave is made. The pictures of Ryan in Mr. Mitchel's book illustrate this to perfection, and there is a passage in the article by Mr. Ryan himself that is worth its weight in gold to the student of hammer throwing.

"A man," says Mr. Ryan, "about to make a throw

should swing the hammer over his head fairly fast, with the shoulders thrown back and the arms held straight out at full length. He should bring the hammer well in front of him before his feet begin to leave the ground for the first turn. At the same time his body should be turning from the hips upward in the direction of the turn. The knees should be slightly bent, so as to impart a little spring to help to throw the body around. It is best to make the first turn as short as a man possibly can and to almost land the feet right behind the stance of the original position. This will give a lot of room for the next two turns and a little leeway to go forward at the spins, for if the thrower cannot go forward his efforts are almost useless. A vital point is to make the slightest pause as the feet touch the ground after the first turn. This will balance the swing and the athlete can tear into the next two like a wild man."

Finally, as to the amount of work to be done, it is obvious that the weight man does not run the same risk of "going stale" as does a sprinter or jumper. Mr. Ryan advises a limit of fifteen throws a day for the beginner, and I dare say that he is right; although I imagine that it all depends on the athlete himself, for personally I used to throw, when learning, much more than this, and with beneficial results.

CHAPTER XIX

THROWING THE FIFTY-SIX POUND WEIGHT

American Amateur Record, 40 ft. 6 3-8 in., M. J. Mc-
Grath, Sept. 23, 1911

THROWING the fifty-six yound weight does not find a place on the programme of the "Intercollegiates," although of recent years it has been included among the field events at the Pennsylvania Relay Carnival. It is, however, one of the regular events at the championships of the Amateur Athletic Union, and is one of the ten events which go to make up the All-around Championship. At first sight the big lead ball appears to be a formidable missile, and for the unskilled beginner there is every chance to expend a huge amount of misdirected energy and constant danger of a strained or pulled muscle. To the performer, however, who understands the art of throwing the weight, it presents no more difficulties than the hammer. Competitors who lack the necessary strength often try to throw the weight from a stand or to revolve once in the circle without swinging the weight around the head, but these methods of throwing are mere makeshifts which cannot result in a throw of any length and the only problems with which we need concern ourselves are throwing the weight with a single and with a double turn.

For the single turn, the theory is exactly the same as in throwing the hammer in the same fashion, except that the greater weight of the fifty-six requires an exaggeration of the principles laid down for the throwing of the lighter weight. The start for the single turn is shown in plate 38.

PLATE 36.
The first swing.

As the weight swings over and behind the right shoulder, the pull exerted is necessarily tremendous, and to counteract this pull and thus prevent the body from being thrown entirely off its balance the athlete must shift his own weight far over on the left leg, and, in addition, a little forward, so that the weight of the body comes upon the ball of the left foot and not upon the heel. In addition, the shoulders must be turned well to the right and the weight must be allowed to swing low over the right shoulder, for keeping the weight well behind the body is absolutely essential for a throw of any length.

PLATE 37.
Just before the turn.

The turn of the body is made exactly as in the case of the hammer. Plate 37 shows the position before the turn, and plate 36 shows both feet on the ground and the weight well behind and under control.

Throwing the fifty-six with a double turn is a problem which need not trouble most athletes, for exceptional size and strength are required to keep control of the weight under these circumstances. The principle is the same as that used in throwing the hammer with a double turn, and is well described by Matt McGrath in his article in "How

THROWING THE FIFTY-SIX POUND WEIGHT

Photo courtesy American Sports Publishing Co.

PLATE 38.

MATT McGRATH.

Start of the "56." First turn.

PLATE 39.
The final effort.

to Become a Weight Thrower." "One swing," says Mr. McGrath, "will be found necessary over the head and this should be nice and loose, the weight traveling well behind the head. As the weight is brought around to the front, the body should wear around with it until the ball is nearly half around the body. Then a little hop is taken and the feet should rest well and firmly on the ground after the first turn. The thrower, if he does as suggested here, may tear into the second turn like a tiger, but he should be careful not to jump too far forward, for if he does he will land over the front of the circle."

CHAPTER XX

THROWING THE DISCUS

American Amateur Record, 156 ft. 1 3-8 in., J. Duncan,
May 27, 1912

Discus throwing was unknown in America until 1896, when the revival of the sport at the Olympic Games, at Athens, and the winning of the event by a member of the American team caused it to be added to the list of athletic sports in this country.

There have been several changes in the method of throwing the discus. According to the Greek rules which were in force at Athens, in 1896, the athlete stood at the back of a six-foot square, facing the direction in which he was to throw. The discus was held in the right hand, with the fingers spread around the edge and the discus resting against the arm. Then a quick step was taken, first with the right and then with the left foot, and the right arm at the same time was swung backward. Then the right leg and the right arm came forward together with much the same motion as that used in the finish of the shot put, and the right wrist was bent forward so that the discus left the fingers in a horizontal position, and scaled through the air in much the same fashion that a clay pigeon is shot from a trap. Under the Greek rules all throws were measured from the point where the discus dropped at right angles to the front of the box, or, if the throw was not made in a straight line, at right angles to the front of the box extended.

PLATE 40.
Throwing the discus. Old style.

Shortly after the discus throw was introduced into America, the rules were changed to permit the throw to be made from a circle seven feet in diameter, and to-day, while the circle has been retained, its diameter has been increased to eight feet, two and one-half inches.

The modern style is to throw with a single turn, but it is interesting to observe that in spite of this resemblance to the hammer and fifty-six, the discus throw is really more like the shot put than like the other weights. A good performer with the shot almost invariably finds little trouble with the discus, while the hammer and fifty-six man

Copyright by Underwood & Underwood.

PLATE 41.

The new style. John Flanagan throwing discus.

often finds difficulty in achieving a good performance with this much lighter weight. Probably the fact that the discus weighs but a trifle over four pounds has something to do with this, but besides this fact, the whole theory of the throw, especially the finish, is really much closer to the shot than to the hammer and fifty-six.

The rudiments of the throw are well described by Mr. James S. Mitchel in his "How to Become a Weight Thrower," when he says, "The most vital part of discus throwing is to learn how to scale it and the proper elevation. First of all it is necessary that the athlete should learn to get a proper hold on the implement, as it conduces to a good method of scaling. In holding the discus it should lie flat against the palm of the hand, with the fingers spread out and the tips covering the outer edge. The thumb should be straightened at an angle of about 45 degrees against the convex part, to steady the missile in making the attempt. Some athletes try to grasp the edge of the disc with the foremost joint of the fingers, but this should be avoided, as it hampers the free use of the arm.

"After the athlete finds he can hold the discus comfortably he should then try a few standing throws. The stationary position is preferred for gaining a line on the proper scaling method. Each day about a dozen trials should be taken this way, after which about as many more should be tried with a turn."

In throwing with a turn, the method is much like that of throwing the hammer with a single turn, with the difference that the position of the body, at the start of the throw, is like that used in the shot put, the athlete facing forward and not with his back to the direction in which he intends to throw. The fundamentals for the athlete to keep in mind are much like those which govern the shot put, namely, that he must not "tighten up" his muscles in the preliminary stages of the throw, that he must not exert too much speed at first, but must save this for the final effort, and that he must not make the throw solely with his arm, but must utilize the full strength of body and legs as well. And in addition to this, the athlete should remember, that as in the hammer, he must not bend or contract the arm while making his swing, but must use a wide, free sweep to get the best results.

CHAPTER XXI

THROWING THE JAVELIN

American Amateur Record, 190 ft., 6 in., G. A. Bronder,
Jr., Sept. 9, 1916

"HONESTY is the best policy," and while I have taken part in practically every event on the athletic programme (I may mention, perhaps, with all due modesty, that I have won prizes in open competition in twenty-five different events), still I must confess that I know practically nothing of throwing the javelin. Therefore, instead of trying to "crib" knowledge from others and pass it off as my own, it seems much better to tell the truth, and to refer my readers to the chapters on the javelin in Michael C. Murphy's "Athletic Training," in Ernest Hjertberg's "Athletics in Theory and Practice," and in James S. Mitchel's "How to Become a Weight Thrower."

At present, because of their long acquaintance with this

sport, the Swedes and Finns easily excel us, but judging from our experience with distance running, with the discus, and with other events where we once lagged behind, but

Photo by Leonard Small, Boston "Globe."
PLATE 42.
Throwing the Javelin. The start.

THROWING THE JAVELIN

have finally come to the front, it seems reasonable to suppose that another ten years may see America competing successfully with the best javelin throwers in the world.

Copyright Underwood & Underwood.

PLATE 43.

Throwing the javelin. The finish. Howard Berry of Pennsylvania.

CHAPTER XXII

THE ALL-AROUND CHAMPIONSHIP

American Amateur Record, 7499 points, F. C. Thomson,
June 5, 1913

THE foregoing chapters have been written with the intention of pointing out the way to proficiency in each particular event, for the average athlete aims to excel in one, two, or, at the most, in three or four events. For those with higher ambitions there remains to be considered the subject of training for the individual all-around championship, often referred to as the "blue ribbon" event of the athletic year.

The term "all-around championship" is certainly no misnomer, for the programme calls for proficiency in every known branch of track and field athletics. The athlete's running powers are tested by the one hundred yards dash, the one hundred and twenty yards hurdle race and the mile run; his jumping abilities by the running high jump, the running broad jump and the pole vault, and his strength and skill at weight throwing by the sixteen-pound shot, the sixteen-pound hammer and the fifty-six pound weight. And, in addition to all this, the program is rounded out by the half-mile walk, an event which is extremely taxing upon the performer.[1] Surely a more complete test could hardly be devised. Speed, spring, strength and endurance—all are necessary, and inability to meet any one of these re-

---

[1] Those interested in walking should consult "Walking for Health and Competition," in Spalding's Athletic Library.

quirements is fatal, since each performance is marked on the scale of one thousand points, the maximum being represented by the world's record in that event, while the minimum is represented by a performance so poor as to be practically within the reach of all.

A light man can hardly hope to become a successful all-around athlete, for while he may do well at the runs and jumps, and may even learn to put the shot creditably, the hammer and the fifty-six pound weight are apt to be a fatal stumbling block. Of course it does not require a giant for these events; but a man should weigh at least one hundred and fifty pounds and should possess strength and science in order to master them.

The all-around athlete is usually a man with a genuine love for athletics, who has spent considerable time not only in training himself, but in watching others perform and in studying the method underlying each event. He must be naturally rugged and able to stand a great deal of work without feeling it, for a very thorough preparation is necessary and it is not an easy task to train for ten different events at the same time. The endurance necessary for the mile run and the half-mile walk, and the strength required to throw the weights well, can only be attained at a sacrifice of speed and spring. On the other hand, light work for the sprints, hurdles and jumps leaves the athlete in good shape for these events, but unable to stand the wear and tear of the long competition.

The best rule in training for the all-around championship is to acquire strength and endurance at any cost. They are absolute requisites to success, and a lay-off for the last week before the competition will bring back much of the spring which may have been diminished by a long period of hard training.

The best volume on all-around work is "All-Around

Athletics," in Spalding's Athletic Library, an excellent summary of the whole subject.

It is very evident that training for the "All-Arounds" is not a task to be undertaken lightly. No one should undertake it unless he has plenty of strength and vitality and takes thorough enjoyment in the work of preparation. On the other hand, if the athlete possesses these requisites the reward is well worth working for. The varied work at the different events builds up all the different muscles and aids wind and limb and if at the conclusion of the period of training the athlete can go through the actual competition with a score of fifty-five hundred points or better, he may well feel that he has attained a good working knowledge of the various branches of track and field athletics.